Dearest Virginia

Dearest Virginia

Love Letters from a Cavalry Officer
in the South Pacific

edited by
Gayle Hunnicutt

KYLE CATHIE LIMITED

For my father, Colonel Sam Lloyd Hunnicutt,

an officer and a gentleman,

and my mother, Mary Virginia Hunnicutt,

the inspiration of these letters

First published in Great Britain in 2004 by
Kyle Cathie Limited
122 Arlington Road
London NW1 7HP
general.enquiries@kyle-cathie.com
www.kylecathie.com

ISBN 1 85626 556 0

© 2004 by Gayle Hunnicutt

Edited by Caroline Taggart
Jacket and layout designed by Button Design plc
Author photograph by Francesca Yorke
Production by Sha Huxtable and Alice Holloway

Gayle Hunnicutt is hereby identified as the author of this work in accordance with
Section 77 of the Copyright, Designs and Patents Act 1988.

A Cataloguing in Publication record for this title is available from the British Library.

Printed in Great Britain by Biddles Ltd, Guildford

Contents

Acknowledgements

In making an acknowledgement the author thanks those people without whom their book could not have been published. My first acknowledgement of thanks is therefore to my father, Colonel Sam Lloyd Hunnicutt. Without his profound and dedicated love for my mother I would not be alive and these letters would not exist. Secondly, I must thank my mother, Virginia Hunnicutt. She is the inspiration for the letters and preserved them for 56 years. Her reminiscences of the lonely vigil she kept while my father was overseas awakened my curiosity and led me to the wooden box in which his 600 letters were carefully stored.

Having read the letters and edited them between January 2001 and February 2003, I then had the remarkable good fortune to meet Kay McCauley. Kay has the exceptional gift of really seeing and listening to people, communicating with them on the deepest level. She gracefully agreed to read the edited letters and then to my astonishment and gratitude asked if she could be my literary agent. Without Kay these letters would be a valuable but private family archive. I met her at the home of my friends Lauro and Julia Martines, whom I would also like to thank.

Through Kay I met Kyle Cathie. She was the only publisher Kay wanted. Kay knew that if Kyle accepted the letters she would make a beautiful book out of them and stand beside it throughout every phase of its publication.

Caroline Taggart has been both my editor and my friend. She has the patience of the proverbial saint and an unerring instinct for content, shape and style. We always saw eye to eye because I quickly learned that Tag knew best 99.9 per cent of the time. On the rare occasions when I felt strongly about a point she readily acquiesced.

Sue Bingham and Joanna Carton of Button Design took the piles of letters and photographs and created the cover and interior layout of *Dearest Virginia*. I could never have envisaged their design, but I knew the minute they sent it to me that it was exactly what I wanted.

The final stage of this process is bringing the book to the attention of the world, and for this I have been put in the care of Julia Barder and Ana Sampson. In my many years as an actress I have never worked with a more efficient or positive publicity team. Their enthusiasm for *Dearest Virginia* and tireless work on its behalf have eased the agony of wondering if anyone is going to buy your book!

I want to thank my aunt, Shirley Hunnicutt, who allowed me to stay in her home in Green Valley, Arizona, for many weeks while I read my father's letters, editing them down from 350,000 words to 138,000. The delicious meals and great companionship she gave me made this project a joy to do and one of my happiest memories.

And finally to Sue Carden of Fort Worth, Texas, my warmest thanks for having the time and patience to type the first draft of these letters. This was an enormous task and she did it with great enthusiasm. Her growing regard for my father as she got to know him through the letters helped me to believe that I was right; that my father's feelings and values throughout the difficult years he spent overseas would speak out to many and should be published.

Gayle's mother's family

| Asa Chapman | + | Nida Love Boaz 'Darlin Love' | | Simon Ghio Dickerson II | + | Mary Elizabeth Hodges |

Laura Belle Chapman   +   Simon Ghio Dickerson III

Mary Virginia Dickerson (Gayle's mother)

Gayle's father's family

| Columbus Jeptha Huffaker | + | Laura Belle Owens | | Samuel Rowel Hunnicutt Senior | + | Frances Merrifield |

Harriet Louise Huffaker 'Hatty Lou'   +   Samuel Rowel Hunnicutt Junior 'Daddy Sam'

Hazel   **Sam Lloyd Hunnicutt**   Jary Jack
(Gayle's father)

Snapshots — a Memoir

Sitting on the floor, surrounded by photographs, I am reconstructing my father's life, a life that eluded me for many years. Not because we weren't close. We were very close. Not because the facts weren't there or because he spent time away from home. He came home every evening. He threw me up in the air and caught me, laughing with his crinkled blue-green eyes which I have inherited. He was Daddy Lloyd and as available to me as any father could be. But was I available to him? Or did I spend much of my seemingly endless childhood reaching out into the world, seeking my own identity through accomplishments and adventures as most young people do? Did I take for granted the lives who devoted their interests to mine; who sacrificed their dreams so I could spread my wings and fly away?

My father made these sacrifices, leaving his first love, the army, so that I could enjoy the more rooted existence of Fort Worth, but he never wanted me to know it. I colluded with him in this unspoken pact until late on the morning of April 18, 1991, when I sat down quietly beside his open coffin and began our farewell conversation.

We had been together in his hospital room laughing and chatting only four days before. He had suddenly smiled and asked, "Where's the boy?" The boy was his nine-year-old grandson, Edward, who had wandered out into the waiting room to look at comic books.

"I'll get him, Daddy," I said.

He wasn't too ill to hold Edward in his arms and spend a few minutes teasing the delighted boy. Daddy was famous for his humour. We were all in good spirits. My father was coming home the next day. Fort Worth, Texas, my home town, was awash with balmy April sunshine, new lime-green leaves on the trees, blazing azaleas and hope. Daddy Lloyd was going to be all right. But he wasn't. He died the next morning of a massive heart attack. He was 83 years old.

My older son, Nolan, flew to Fort Worth to be with us. I left the two boys to look after my mother and, still in a state of shock, found myself sitting alone beside my father in the funeral home. To my surprise, I heard myself say aloud, "Daddy, I'm sorry you made so many sacrifices for me. I know you never resented them. But now I realize that I have the life I dreamed of because of those sacrifices and I shall never forget it. I'm going to miss you so, so much."

I couldn't have known then just how much I would miss my father when, over the next ten years, my own life became blurred from time to time with disillusionments. He had set a standard for me of integrity, honesty and unselfishness which blinded me to reality, at least to the reality of the world I moved into when I left the safety of my home and friends in Fort Worth.

I first embarked upon this reconstruction of my father's life in March 1999. I was in the throes of a four-day marathon, clearing out the home my parents shared for the last 30 years of their 55-year marriage. During this blitz of sorting and packing up their possessions, choosing what to sell, what to give away and, most importantly, what to keep and ship back home to London, I discovered a tightly packed box of old letters, letters which had been carefully preserved and locked in the garage closet with Mother's best silver, porcelain and jewellery. Although my policy was never to stop and read anything except briefly to ascertain its worth, I was drawn to these letters. Carefully pulling out four or five, all written in my father's distinctive hand, I began to read. I soon recognized that in this box were hundreds and hundreds of letters that he had written my mother from the South Pacific during World War II. I couldn't stop reading. Finally as the heat in the garage became stifling, I carefully repacked them and decided to hand-carry them back to London, expecting to devour them the moment I returned. But life intervened and the letters sat in the bottom of my closet for many months.

Occasionally my mother would ask over the telephone if I had begun reading the letters. We had a plan that I would read them all and then bring photocopies back to Fort Worth where she was safely installed in a nursing home which we had chosen together. These letters were the only mementoes of that strangely happy yet frightening period of her life when she was carrying her first and only child while her husband fought boredom, loneliness, mosquitoes and from time to time the Japanese between July 1942 and July 1944.

Then one dark November day, like a magnet, the letters pulled me towards the closet door. The person I needed most in my life at that time was my father. I knew his quiet decency and delightful humour would be contained in those letters. And so it proved.

Who was Sam Lloyd Hunnicutt? Only when you try to capture in words someone you knew for forty-seven years, someone whose life was inextricably bound up with yours, do you feel the elusive nature of your endeavour. Will you convey the warmth of his voice, the timing of his jokes, the graceful resignation of his later years? So much of my father's inner reality is contained in these letters that I view my job as that of the narrator, the person who sets the scene and fills in the gaps better to illuminate the world in which he lived and from which he formed his beliefs. I would like you to see him as a boy, a university student suddenly hit by the Depression, a father and a grandfather, the role I believe he enjoyed best.

The handsome mounted cavalry officer of 32 whom you will meet in these letters stood on the railway platform in El Paso, Texas in July, 1942 and waved farewell to his adored wife, Virginia, his domineering mother, Hatty Lou, and his vivacious older sister, Hazel. The troop train bound for San Francisco pulled out of the station. It was seven months after the Japanese bombing of Pearl Harbor. The men were heading for the South Pacific. That moment of farewell has been described to me many times by my mother, now aged 94. She is blessed with the Southern lady's love of family stories and an excellent memory. "Honey, I'm afraid your grandmother just bawled like a sick cow all the way home to Fort Worth." Hatty Lou Huffaker Hunnicutt suffered from high blood pressure and "nerves". Although I remember her with a permanent crease in her brow and a sense of disquiet, so unlike my Dickerson grandmother, who was always smiling and gentle, I know from the many family photographs I have inherited that Hatty Lou was once a delicate beauty. Even as a young mother sitting on a shabby front porch with her children, Hazel and Lloyd, she has an air of mystery.

That porch was in Galveston, a bustling Texas seaport where my grandparents were living. Although brought up with cattle, Sam Rowel Hunnicutt had got a good job with the Santa Fe Railroad as the division freight agent. Perhaps they would have stayed in Galveston if the hurricane of 1915 hadn't forced them to flee. They were, in fact, the last car across the main bridge before it was swept away by an enormous wave. The family returned to Fort Worth, still known as Cowtown, the last provisioning post on the Chisholm Trail and the place where the West begins. My grandfather decided to return to his first love, the cattle business, and established the Hunnicutt

ABOVE: Hatty Lou Hunnicutt, my grandmother, a displaced "belle", outside her first home in Texas.

ABOVE: Sam Rowel Hunnicutt, Jr., my grandfather (on the right). He is about to sell his prize bull, which weighed 1985 lb, at the Fort Worth Stock Yards.

Hatty Lou with Hazel, Lloyd and Hatty Lou's sister-in-law, Aunt Julia. The rocking chair on the right now resides in my kitchen in London.

Livestock Commission. They bought a home on Pearl Street close by the stockyards.

Hazel secretly decided that before she left high school the family would move to the more prestigious Southside so that she could graduate from Southside High School, now known as Paschal, my old alma mater. She wanted to come from the right side of the tracks. Lloyd was happy hanging around the stockyards talking to the cowboys coming in off the trail drives and helping out his dad. I have a photograph showing Sam Rowel with his partner selling a bull which weighed 1,985 pounds, a record for that time in Fort Worth. Texans are big talkers with expansive, hospitable natures who don't know a stranger. Lloyd was often seen after school enjoying this camaraderie, sitting on a split rail fence, "chawing" with his friends.

But Hatty Lou had other plans for her son. He must learn the importance of work, of saving every penny, of never wasting time. He was certainly not going to hang out with boys who chewed tobacco and said "meealk" rather than milk. From the age of ten Lloyd had to get up at 4 a.m. to deliver newspapers. Then he would rush home, milk the family cow, collect the eggs from the hen house, do his other chores, change into his school clothes and dash to class, often not having enough time for breakfast.

Sam Hunnicutt had been quite a catch for Hatty Lou, whose father, Columbus Jeptha Huffaker, owned the livery stable in Greenville, Texas. Sam's father, also named Sam Hunnicutt, was one of the biggest cattle ranchers in those parts and the Hunnicutt home in Greenville was imposing. Sam junior and Hatty Lou made a handsome couple. She must have felt that her future was secure when they married on September 24th, 1903.

Shortly after this, however, Sam senior lost nearly his entire herd in a flash flood, an event from which his fortunes never recovered. Perhaps this explains a snapshot I have of Hatty Lou wearing an elegant turn-of-the-century dress with a high lace collar, tightly belted waist and long lace skirt, carrying a parasol over her head to protect her skin from the scorching Texas sun. She looks like a "belle". But behind her is a shack-like house on a dirt prairie. Was this the home she and Sam shared in their early marriage? Surely they had come down in the world. Perhaps this is what ate into her soul and caused her to drive her children ruthlessly in an attempt to regain their lost position.

Both of Hatty Lou and Sam's boys were dark-haired and sweet-natured. Hazel was also dark-haired and had flashing green eyes. She was always stubborn. She learned how to get her way with enormous charm and a vivacious personality which she later taught to the budding young debutantes of Fort Worth along with piano lessons. My favourite childhood portrait of Hazel captures these qualities. Her head is cocked, her mouth set, her stance defiant. My father's earliest photographs show a serious little boy who must have suffered much from his overwhelming sister.

Hazel was the star of the family, a petite fireball who could "magic" any room. Lloyd was a loner. His chores at home kept him so busy that he never had time to learn sport like the other boys at Southside High. He hadn't seen the latest movie because he gave all his earnings to his mother to help the family finances. Like so many lonely children he lost himself in books.

Lloyd's other lifelong passion was for horses. He loved riding them, training them, grooming them. To me, no man could have looked more handsome than my father mounted on his palomino, Sun Up, as he led his troops across the military parade ground. Did Lloyd ever dream of that moment when he was a boy? Possibly. The dreams of young children often project them into the reality of their adult lives.

I know from his letters to my mother that he had learned early on to pretend not to care about things he couldn't have. But after he fell in love with Virginia, a world of new interests began to open up for him. Her passion for bridge, which was wildly fashionable with the smart young set, was the only exception. "People who play bridge don't read books," he pronounced.

ABOVE: Miss Hazel Hunnicutt, aged three, with her determined character fully formed and on show.

LEFT: Lloyd, Hazel and Jary Jack Hunnicutt, the "Hunni Kids", sitting in a wheelbarrow on Pearl Street, the Northside, Fort Worth.

ABOVE: The "Hunni Kids", grown up and eating candy in the breakfast room on Irwin Avenue, the Southside, Fort Worth.

RIGHT: Petite Hazel and long, lanky Lloyd in their late teens on Pearl Street, just before the family made their escape to the more affluent Southside.

My mother came from two long-established Southern families. Her father, Simon Ghio Dickerson, who seems to have been born with a book in his hand, was a Virginian. His family moved to Forth Worth after the American Civil War or the "War between the States" as many Southerners still call it. Her mother, Laura Belle Chapman, was a Georgian and met Simon, a distant cousin, in Calhoun, Georgia where they were both guests at a family wedding. For these Southerners, brought up with all the comforts of a grand plantation and its retinue of servants, Texas was a great shock. Their way of life that been destroyed, but the dream of the old South, a part-real, part-mythical world of old-fashioned courtesy and graceful living, remained deep inside them and contrasted harshly with the rough and ready pioneer world of the West. "Oh honey, I can't bear this hot, dusty old Texas," my grandmother Laura Belle would say to me as she sat on the front porch in her rocker pouring ice tea or fresh lemonade for neighbours who dropped by to pass the time of day. My treat was an ice-cold Coke in a frozen beer stein and on special occasions a Coke float made with home-made vanilla ice cream.

The kind hospitable ladies who dropped by to visit Laura Belle never worked at anything except cooking and washingup three meals a day, running their houses and raising their children. In Texas, plantation staff was singularly lacking. By today's standards their lives were a "non-existence", although they seemed content, fulfilled and to have time for others, a quality many modern women lack.

They were gracious ladies. "Pretty if you can, but pleasant if it kills you" was their motto. Their generosity to family and friends was legendary. Even the most remote cousin was welcomed as a person of great family importance. Cousinage in the Old South has always been a dominant theme and many hours can be spent establishing whether Hodges was the second cousin or first cousin once removed of Charles Boaz who was great-grandmother's brother and had "the prettiest horses in Georgia".

When the railroads opened up the West after the Civil War many Southern families cut their losses and in time-honoured American tradition decided to move out and start all over again where the future held hope for prosperity in the land of the free and the brave. The railroad companies themselves offered job opportunities, and Simon Ghio's father secured one of the best, enabling him to settle his family of six in comfort on the elegant Elizabeth Boulevard in Fort Worth.

Throughout my childhood I sat at my grandmother's feet on my special needlepoint stool as she told stories of plantation life with its leisurely pace, delicious food, cotillion balls, exhilarating fox hunts, romantic moonlit rides on the finest thoroughbred horses and festive trips to New Orleans. She once heard the cry of a black panther in the Everglades of Florida. Who would not miss such a life?

The Hunnicutts, like the Dickersons, were originally English. They were pioneers from Tennessee with a family mythology which revolved around their descent from the great huntsman and Indian tracker, Daniel Boone. Robert Hunnicutt, born in 1760 in South Carolina, served in the Revolutionary War. His son, William Hunnicutt, was born in Virginia in 1790 but moved with his parents to Giles County, Tennessee which was then frontier country. William married a Miss Joanna Barber, also originally of Virginia. He was a "strictly temperate man" and served as Justice of the Peace in Giles County for many years. Of their seven children only Winfield Scott Hunnicutt survived and it was he who moved to Texas in the fall of 1850. Having invested in land he soon became a prosperous rancher.

Texas was far less of a threat to these hearty people, although in the 1890s it was rough and ready by anyone's standards. Butch Cassidy and the Sundance Kid hid out in Fort Worth with their infamous Hole in the Wall gang. The stockyards, cotton yards, wagon yards, dry goods stores, saloons and dirt-packed streets filled with horse-drawn buggies and covered wagons could absorb many outlaws.

As I look back on these lives, I see three facts clearly. My aunt, Hazel Hunnicutt, was determined that she was going to transcend her humble beginnings and establish herself as a leading light in Fort Worth. My father, Lloyd Hunnicutt, was going to escape the tyranny of his mother by joining the US Army, which would fill his life with a sense of belonging and the excitement his youth so often lacked. My mother, Virginia Dickerson, was going to remain a gracious Southern lady, which she is to this day.

Virginia's parents were more relaxed than the Hunnicutts and did not plan aggressively for her future. She was president of her high school sorority, formed a successful bridge club, travelled to Georgia and Virginia to visit cousins and attended secretarial college. They assumed she would meet a nice intelligent man in a few years' time and marry him, which she did.

Hatty Lou Hunnicutt was an interventionist. She had plans for her children, lots of plans. Receiving a university education was high on the list of "musts". She had been denied this opportunity. Hazel therefore attended the University of Missouri where she pledged the most sought-after sorority. She was always popular with men and with women. Hazel knew how to dazzle while remaining unattainable, an almost impossible feat in today's society. Lloyd attended TCU (Texas Christian University) in Fort Worth and lived at home until his junior year when he persuaded his parents to send him to A & M (Texas Agricultural and Mechanical College). Jary Jack, born ten years after Lloyd, was still the adored "baby".

None of these young people could have anticipated the devastation of 1929 when the Great Depression hit. Hazel was ordered home from university to help the family survive by teaching piano lessons and "charm". She left behind her true love, whose memory haunted the rest of her life. Lloyd had to drop out of A & M and go to work at Swift & Co, a large meat-packing company. He learned the job from the gristly bottom up.

In such difficult times it may seem strange that anyone had the money to pay for piano lessons, let alone charm. But there were still enormously wealthy oil families whose fortunes were intact. The vastness of this wealth cannot be exaggerated. Oil and Texas have always been synonymous. Once their gushers came in, the oil families wanted to spend their money on refinements and becoming cultured, one of Hazel's favourite words when she became the Professor of Personality at Texas Wesleyan College. These hard-working, wild-catting entrepreneurs soon realized that their progeny could be moulded into shape by the petite, vivacious Hazel. She then expanded this tutelage of piano lessons and charm into the more expansive programme of taking her teenage "chicks", as she called them, on a European Grand Tour. Her first trip was in the summer of 1948 as the world began to recover from the devastation of World War II.

But I have travelled twenty years into the future. In 1929 the yardstick by which the Hunnicutt family measured the sudden violent reversal of fortune caused by the Depression was the oft-repeated phrase of my childhood, "You know, Daddy Sam didn't even have a dime for the streetcar. He had to walk five miles to the stockyards and five miles back." I wonder if Daddy Sam secretly wished he was still living on Pearl Street ten minutes walk from the stockyards on the Northside?

Although the Dickersons were not as hard hit as the Hunnicutts, Virginia decided she would use her secretarial skills and get a job at Swift & Co. She began as the receptionist and worked her way up to being private secretary to Mr Platt, the plant manager. Lloyd was now one of Swift's leading salesmen. He breezed in one day to discuss a new contract with Mr Platt and was struck by the beautiful young lady sitting in the outer office fielding her boss's calls and visitors. On the way out he asked for her phone number and then rang every day for a week, inviting Virginia to dinner. Every day she refused him, as brought-up girls did. Finally, on the seventh day, his persistence prevailed. They went with another couple to Mineral Wells, an hour's drive

*Virginia and Lloyd Hunnicutt as newlyweds
on his National Guard cavalry manoeuvres at
Fort Riley, Kansas, 1937.*

Captain Sam Lloyd Hunnicutt
with his dog, Blackie; carrying
supplies on the base; admiring his
bride, Virginia; and riding his
prize-winning stallion, Sun Up,
at Fort Riley, Kansas.

from Fort Worth, where they dined and danced on the roof terrace of the legendary Baker Hotel. Lloyd was very funny and a wonderful dancer. That night was their beginning and "it was fireworks from then on," my mother remembers. The feelings they shared that night still pulsed in her veins 67 years later.

Until I read my father's letters, I never realized that they had eloped in October 1936. After the service in the Episcopal Chapel in Weatherford, Texas, my mother rang her parents to tell them the news. They were delighted, immediately welcoming Lloyd into the family. When my father rang home, his mother had a fit and insisted that they would not be properly married until the service had been performed by "her" minister at First Methodist Church. On New Year's Day 1937 this service was duly conducted and Hatty Lou's fury at having been left out of such an important family occasion was now assuaged. January 1st was the anniversary they always celebrated, possibly because it was easy to remember, although my father's romantic nature and love of giving presents make me believe that he would never have forgotten such a significant day.

My parents' married life began in army quarters on a military base. My mother soon discovered that she adored army life. Here she found a ready-made society of other young couples who shared her interests. She could admire her handsome husband when he returned home on a hot summer's evening in his military whites having been on parade before a visiting general. Banquets and ballroom dances were held on the post almost every Saturday night and my parents were often the hit of the evening as they whirled in perfect harmony across the polished dance floor. My mother would wear a mid-calf length cocktail dress and cocktail hat. My father wore his impeccably cut dress uniform. They were a "wow", I was told as a girl.

The war was three years away and life was sweet. The only unhappiness that crept into those years was the uneasy feeling that they might not be able to have a child. Virginia had experienced several miscarriages and after the last painful

Fort Worth Star Telegram newspaper clippings celebrating my parents' marriage on January 1, 1937, the society wedding insisted on by Hatty Lou.

episode my parents began to give up hope. The Hunnicutts were desperate for a grandchild and my mother felt she was failing them. Most of all she simply wanted a child who would be the outcome of her deeply passionate love for my father. After a few years they quit speaking of these hopes.

Would I have been born if Daddy hadn't gone to war? My mother was two months' pregnant when he went overseas. I sometimes think she willed her body to conceive in case the war took my father away from her. She never did so again.

My father's war years have become known to me only through reading these letters. Like many returning soldiers he almost never discussed his experiences, although he remained active in the military throughout my childhood. Lloyd left Fort Worth a healthy, dashing young officer. He returned with his sense of humour intact but his skeletal body wracked with malaria and his skin a bright yellow from taking Atabrine, the anti-malaria medication of the day. My mother met him after a separation of two years in El Paso, Texas and burst into tears in their hotel room. She pretended her tears were from joy but they were actually from shock. He regained the lost weight and normal skin colour but his nerves were "shot". For a number of years he was restless and distracted, chasing freight trains in his car and clambering over steam locomotives when he felt too pent up. I loved these adventures and never realized what lay behind them.

For me Daddy Lloyd was always a hero. He was like a character in a play about whom the other characters speak a great deal before they make their entrance. I was 18 months old when my parents pulled up outside the house on Irwin in a pale blue coupé after their private reunion in El Paso. Having given every member of his family a carefully wrapped present brought back from the South Pacific, he took me out on the side veranda so we could have some time alone together. He later told my mother that as he started to rock the porch swing I said, "Be careful, Daddy. Don't rock me too hard. I might fall down and hurt myself". I learned throughout my childhood that my father would never do anything to hurt me, that he would make me feel loved my entire life.

We were a military family of three, plus a small cocker spaniel named Pudgey. Our quarters were comfortable and my vague memories, stirred by family snapshots, are happy ones. One event, however, did darken this idyllic time. My mother, an excellent horsewoman, decided to join Daddy and his new unit of soldiers on an exercise. Daddy put her on a large, half-broken horse which she had ridden before and liked. He then warned his men of the horse's one dangerous flaw. He could not bear another horse to get in front of him. The ride went well until they came to a busy highway crossing. While waiting for the traffic to subside one of the men lost control of his horse and dashed ahead of my mother's. With all her skill there was nothing she could do. The horse had the bit in his teeth and raced away. She held on praying he wouldn't swerve to the right into the oncoming traffic or to the left into a steep gully. He did neither. He headed home to the stable. Relieved, she was poised to take the fence surrounding the stable yard when the horse baulked. Mother flew into the air and landed on her back. She was stunned and then realized she couldn't move.

Lloyd was leading his men back slowly in case another horse got away. Mother lay on the ground in agony. The incident was the turning point in their life together. Mother's back mended but only after months of bed rest and chronic pain for which she needed strong painkillers. Daddy decided some six months later to leave the army and return to Fort Worth, where there would be a family support system for my mother and me. She never wanted him to leave the army and, as each of his attempts at business failed, I believe he grew to regret that critical decision. Thankfully he remained in the National Reserves where his career continued to flourish, culminating in a succession of promotions, finally becoming the Commandant of the Fort Worth National Reserve Unit where he ended his career teaching the strategy of nuclear war. The progression from cavalry to nuclear war has always struck me as a long leap in one man's military career.

Hatty Lou and Hazel believed that growing up in Fort Worth was of vital importance so that one day I could take my place in Fort Worth society. The old atavistic urge to live on the right side of the tracks had never died, and they were thrilled to have more control of the only family grandchild. The Dickersons were simply pleased to have the young family so nearby.

Daddy after the war as Commandant of the 4159th Reserve Forces School. He was promoted to full colonel in the reserves and at 78 received a commendation from President Reagan for his life-long services to the US Army.

RIGHT: A family portrait taken around the piano on Irwin Avenue. This piano saved the Hunnicutts from destitution in the Depression and was used by Hazel to teach music until she reached her eighties. My mother, on the far right, looks excluded and strained.

Miss Gayle Hunnicutt evolves into a young lady, her dresses handmade by Hatty Lou or purchased with fanfare by Hazel from the impossibly glamorous Neiman Marcus store if she learned her piano pieces well.

Hatty's blood pressure was becoming a serious problem and her strategy of "taking to her bed" was now based on real need. She died at age 64. My mother told me that she only discovered what a delightful conversationalist my grandfather was when his wife passed away. I remember him as the best of cooks, a good bedtime storyteller and a reassuring presence in his wicker rocker next to the fireplace when he sat at all family gatherings peacefully smoking his pipe.

Growing up in Fort Worth was enormous fun. At school we were always encouraged to learn in a positive way, for pleasure and for self-esteem. If you had an attentive father who made flash cards to help you master maths and trained you to win the spelling bee, you enjoyed school even more. Simo and Lala, which is what I called my Dickerson grandparents, were great readers and steered me into the early delights of *The Bobbsey Twins, Uncle Wiggily, The Wizard of Oz, Nancy Drew* mystery stories, *Alice in Wonderland, David Copperfield* and *Treasure Island*. I learned from my mother several years ago that Simo read all twelve volumes of Proust cover to cover four different times in his life. I wish I could discuss them with him now.

Hazel's annual trip to Europe, her Grand Tour, happened every summer for thirty years from 1948. One of my clearest memories is the sight of the Hunnicutt dining table covered in Hazel's elegant and perfectly folded clothes. She started this process at least a month before her departure, adding and subtracting items until she had the perfect wardrobe for her two-month trip. She always travelled first class and looked stunning in Chanel suits, Katharine Hepburn trousers, stylish hats and feminine cocktail dresses.

Her enormous success with her "chicks" I have only come to understand as an adult. She could walk further, visit more museums, get up earlier, stay up later and laugh more infectiously than any of the 16-year-olds and they adored her for it. They wanted to please her and therefore behaved well because for all her vivacity, Hazel was strict. She allowed no swearing, no

A sparkling Miss Hazel Hunnicutt in the 1920s. Her magnetic personality drew everyone to her, except, perhaps, my mother.

Hazel with her "chicks" aboard the first civilian crossing of the Cunard liner the Queen Mary from New York to Southampton after the war.

smoking, no drinking and certainly no "S…E…X". The parents of Fort Worth paid well for such supervision and guidance.

This sense of values is what I miss most about my childhood. Both the Hunnicutts and Dickersons were ethical, church-going families and had strong views on what was acceptable and what was unacceptable behaviour. Moral ambiguity and personal irresponsibility were unknown to them. They were true blue. They didn't lie, deceive, cheat or betray. They were decent, transparent people with good manners which didn't mask dark secrets or grimy realities. My mother still shines with these values. The good manners of most Texans I know are little acts of kindness designed to put other people at ease and make them feel good about themselves.

Goodness, which flows from a real desire to help others, is as healing as the warmth of the sun. I learned this from my father, who followed the tradition of many Americans by giving time to his family and to his community. Those who are able to do so share their wealth as well as their time. We give what we can. Although my father's life in business never matched his hopes for success, he was at peace. He always retained the dignity of a Southern gentleman without a note of falseness. And he still loved chasing trains. My sons, Nolan and Edward, revelled in these madcap adventures. "Put on your galoshes, boys. We're going to a train wreck and it will be muddy!" was a cry to delight the heart of any young adventurer.

My only worry about Daddy's influence on Nolan and Edward was his addiction to giant gumdrops. He had a passion for them and I'm sure this was shared with Nolan and Edward when I wasn't watching. He would line up one of each colour (usually seven in all) and place them in a neat row on the table next to his armchair. As he read his book after supper he ate the gumdrops one at a time with great satisfaction. One evening, however, he placed not seven but fourteen gumdrops on the table. As they slowly disappeared my mother, in some astonishment, asked why he was eating so many. He replied with a chuckle, "Oh, I have a test for diabetes in the morning and I thought I'd give Dr Childs a scare."

Noone who has ever been to my hometown and met the locals could fail to notice how gracious and hospitable these people are, or how beautifully they maintain their Ante-Bellum, Colonial, Early American, Spanish, English, French or Post-Modernist houses. Visitors are surprised to discover that Fort Worth is a green, tree-laden town with the Trinity River running through it, having expected the dry, flat scenery of the Texas Panhandle which is actually hundreds of miles northwest.

Although my parents lived in a modest house, they loved driving through the fine residential areas of Fort Worth and the countryside which surrounds them. They didn't stop their ritual of a leisurely Sunday afternoon drive until my father was in his mid-seventies. When I was young we attended First Methodist Church at eleven in the morning with Hazel and my grandfather. We then joined friends at Colonial Country Club (membership was another of Hazel's social triumphs) for the Sunday buffet with its vast array of irresistible food. Large ice carvings of swans, softly lit from within, decorated the three buffet tables.

After lunch we embarked on our drive. Daddy might head for Granbury to see the fine town square and old courthouse, crossing beautiful stretches of prairie to get there. But our favourite drive was through the lush Fort Worth residential areas of Rivercrest and Westover. My parents would pick out different aspects of the houses they most admired and debate how these features would fit into their own dream house, a house Daddy had started planning in the South Pacific and frequently referred to in his letters home. They were never able to build that house, but they spent many happy hours planning it.

Gradually my parents' life became centred more and more on their home. They read, listened to music and watched their favourite television programmes. They greatly looked forward to our visits from England, where I moved in 1969 after my marriage to the English actor David Hemmings. My sons would start the day by devouring American cartoons. I read my book with occasional furtive peeks at the screen while Daddy made our breakfast of turtle-shaped pancakes, crispy bacon, sausages and eggs. After breakfast he liked to drink his coffee, smoke a cigarette and read the newspaper thoroughly. We raced around Fort Worth in the car seeing friends and running errands.

Most of these trips happened in April or July, but occasionally we got home for Christmas. In London I am teased to this day about the size of the Christmas tree I choose, the amount of

lights I put on it and the abundance of ornaments. To an English eye my Christmas tree probably looks quite vulgar, but to me it is a tribute to the hours my father and I spent together decorating the biggest, bushiest tree he could find.

Christmas was important. Mother and Daddy each took enormous trouble when choosing gifts, trying to find something which would be useful but also an exciting surprise. My presents were requested in a letter to Santa Claus. I realize now that my parents must have struggled to save for these gifts as my tastes were conditioned by having wealthy friends. I feel sure no young girl ever received a more beautiful doll than I did on Christmas morning in 1953. She was a Madame Alexandra Queen Doll, a replica of the young Queen Elizabeth II. Her filigree lace ballgown,

One of Daddy Lloyd's first Christmases at home after he returned from the South Pacific. My parents' huge enjoyment of Christmas was typical of their total lack of cynicism about life, and helped me to see the world as a magical, welcoming place.

edged in the faintest gold over peach satin and crossed with a
pale blue sash on which rested a diamond brooch, imparted a
dignity and beauty of nearly divine status to my young eyes. She
is still with me, although her head rests beside her in the storage
box in which she has been living for the past 45 years. I suspect
she will be mended now that I have my first granddaughter.

For my birthday the following February Mother designed a
white peau de soie ballgown for my Madame Alexandra doll. The
soft white fabric was broken only by a cranberry-red satin belt,
crushed as it encircled the waist, then fanning out into an
enormous bow at the back with wide streamers reaching down
to the ground. The design of the bodice was simple with a
scoop neck and off-the-shoulder sleeves. When I was 16,
I attended my first Steeplechase ball with a 17-year-old beau
whose sister was a debutante that year. I wore an exact replica
of my doll's creamy white gown. I can't pretend I looked anything
like my queen doll, being still at an awkward age, part teenager,
part young woman, but I did find the evening incredibly
glamorous as we waltzed and danced the fox trot, rumba,
mambo and samba. We had been taught these dances in our
ballroom classes on Park Hill Drive. I wanted to live up to my
parents' reputation for tripping the light fantastic. And Hazel was
going to be at the same party, sashaying across the dance floor
in her inimitable style. Fort Worth would be en fête.

During the 34 years I have lived in England I have attended
many lovely parties, dances and galas, but I have never seen
any which could rival the splendour of a Fort Worth
extravaganza. These evenings are the stage-set for the
important ritual of presenting to society the young ladies of Fort
Worth's most prominent families. As their parents beam with
pride the fledgling beauties make their sweeping curtsies to the
floor, supported by an often tall, handsome Texas boy from a
good family. He might be attending Harvard or Yale, but is more
likely a student at the University of Texas, an institution of which
Texans are justifiably proud.

Once the Thanksgiving rituals of the Steeplechase and
Assembly balls are completed the private parties of the season
begin, lasting until Christmas. A spirit of friendly competition
prevails as country-club swimming pools are drained and
covered over to become enormous dance floors. Private jets
whizz back and forth from Fort Worth to New York as excited
girls choose their festive frocks.

I have memories of many of these dances, but several stand
out as especially glamorous. One family took the Olympic-sized
swimming pool at Ridglea Country Club, covered it with
translucent squares and placed a light under each panel,
creating the impression of an enormous multi-coloured jewel
surrounded by arbours in which elegant tables for ten were
swathed in shimmering shot-silk, the candelabras festooned in
cascading flowers. The scent of mimosa filled the air and every
place was marked by a beautifully wrapped gift in which each
guest found a small diamond finger-ring or gold cufflinks. At a
Black and Red Ball the guests were invited to come masked as
Venetians at Carnival. A Snow Ball transported Fort Worthians
back to Tsarist Russia. Perhaps the most spectacular of all was
the Magnolia Ball, at which an enormous tree, placed in the
foyer of the country club, was created entirely out of magnolia
blossoms – an unforgettable sight.

Of course these debutantes were lovely girls, but they
must also be cultured and Hazel Hunnicutt's European tour
did the trick. No one who has grown up in London can
imagine how it feels for a young Texan to see the Houses of
Parliament for the first time illuminated on a glistening night in
June. As you swirl in a coach from the Southampton boat
train to the Ritz Hotel, the heart beats quickly. London,
Stratford, Gloucestershire and eight European countries were
about to unfold before the awe-struck travellers. However
grand the houses are in Fort Worth, they can never match the
fairy-tale reality of an ancient castle lived in by a genuine earl
or duke in the eyes of a 16-year-old girl.

ABOVE: David
Hemmings and Gayle
Hunnicutt on their
wedding day, November
16, 1968, in a rose garden
in Beverly Hills,
California.

RIGHT: The newlyweds
about to depart for their
honeymoon in Acapulco,
sharing a final joke with
Daddy Lloyd.

Did Hazel ever imagine what an important seed she was sowing when she took me to Europe with her in 1960? Did my parents realize when I received my scholarship to the University of California (UCLA) that I would never live at home again, however many times I might visit over the years? They never once complained and were always eager to listen to my plans for the future. I think they were secretly pleased I didn't stay in Fort Worth to run the Hazel Hunnicutt Travel Agency.

Mother didn't like to travel after her riding accident, but when I married David Hemmings in 1968 my father flew to Los Angeles, where I was working hard to establish myself as an actress. David was already an experienced actor at the age of 26 and had been a child opera singer, touring Europe with the composer Benjamin Britten in his haunting opera *The Turn of the*

BELOW LEFT: Gayle and David with their much-loved baby boy, Nolan Christopher David Hemmings, on Hutton Drive, Beverly Hills, 1971
BELOW RIGHT: Daddy Lloyd in the cottage hospital, St Asaph, North Wales, admiring his newborn grandson.

Screw. When Antonioni's film *Blow-Up*, in which David starred, won the Palme d'Or at the Cannes Film Festival that year, David became famous all over the world. No young actor can perceive how unusual such phenomenal success is and how rarely it happens in a career, if at all. Catching the zeitgeist of the Sixties and "swinging London", this now-revered film also celebrated the newly realized power of youth and the transition of photography to an art form. Fascinating filmgoers today and studied in film schools, it has lost none of its power to intrigue.

For these two young people about to be married under garlands of flowers in the rose garden of a white colonial house in Beverly Hills, whose swimming pool was adorned with pale pink and lavender doves, the excitement of *Blow-Up* was what happened in Hollywood. Surely life would always be like this,

Life as a young film star: at Heathrow, waiting for a flight home to Texas; and speeding through the Pacific Ocean at Malibu Colony.

ABOVE: *A photograph that appeared in
the London Evening Standard on the
day Simon and I announced our
engagement in the spring of 1978.*

ABOVE: *The bridal
party processing
from the Grosvenor
Chapel, London,
to their wedding
reception, held in
a private garden
behind South
Audley Street,
September 15, 1978.*

*Three-year-old Edward Lloyd Jenkins with his
parents at their home in Primrose Hill, London.*

wouldn't it? Didn't everyone have Henry Mancini organize the music for their wedding, and the Mamas and the Papas perform a spontaneous song-fest after dinner? We were so young and so naive. My father took it more in his stride. He enjoyed our friends, who were welcoming film people, and they enjoyed him.

One of my fondest memories is of Daddy seated next to the film star Steve McQueen at the wedding dinner. Steve was the most drop-dead gorgeous man I've ever met, but once the heart recovered from its mini-swoon, there was the problem of conversation. You had to know a great deal about motorcycles, sports cars or engines to avoid embarrassing silences. My father, however, was fine. Steve, it turned out, was steeped in American war history in Asia, having just completed his film *The Sand Pebbles*, and Daddy began to relive his experiences in New Caledonia and New Guinea. That was a rare occurrence. They chatted away. Any worries I had that my father might be over-awed by the exotic world of which I had temporarily become a part were unfounded. My father liked people wherever he met them. He was a straight-shooting, no-bullshit Texan with the courtesy and charm of a Southern gentleman. That combination is hard to beat.

Hazel was able to visit London for my second marriage, to the British journalist and writer Simon Jenkins. My father sadly wasn't. His old enemy malaria and the effects of age were slowing him down. Simon and I always chuckle when we remember the evening his parents took us all to dinner at the Athenaeum Club just before the wedding. I watched Hazel like a hawk, but in the library, while Simon and I went to get coffee for the five of us, she triumphed. With tears gently welling up, she took my mother-in-law-to-be's hand and pronounced, "We are so grateful to Simon for marrying Gayle. After all, she is a divorced woman!" Nell had to struggle hard to repress her mirth, having a more robust and pragmatic attitude to life.

The blessing service which followed our registry office wedding was held on a warm, sunny Friday afternoon, September 15, 1978. The Grosvenor Chapel was full of old friends and new, Monteverdi's music, great sprays of flowers and the time-honoured vows of love and commitment. Afterwards we all processed to the house of a friend which was only a short walk away, where we entered the communal garden tucked away behind these dignified eighteenth-century houses. There, under a marquee filled with lilies, our marriage was celebrated with much gaiety and some rather good speeches. For me, that day was a swirl of happiness.

~ ∾ ~

As I sit typing this memoir in my London home, where I have lived with Simon for 25 years, I feel a great sense of place and stability. I love my adopted country. And yet there is always a current running beneath this contentment, a current of longing for Texas, for Fort Worth, for the dynamism and generosity of my family and friends there, for their goodness and transparency. The poignancy most of us experience when we remember the past is a part of getting older. Perhaps it's more intense when you no longer live in your own country. These letters, which I have read many times over, have helped assuage that longing. They have also enabled me to get to know my father as a man in his early thirties. The unconditional love he felt for my mother, his high ideals of honour, his sense of duty and pride in his country plus that dry, zany sense of humour delight me to this day.

My father was reassuringly predictable. He always enjoyed barbecue, making stews and chasing trains. He gave his love unstintingly to his wife, his daughter and his grandsons. He was a true Texan. He enjoyed Fort Worth and was glad it was his home. He was Colonel Sam Lloyd Hunnicutt, and I am proud of being his daughter and of carrying his name. In times of despair, my father's example of leading an honourable life while still having enormous fun has kept me going. These letters reaffirm my faith in that philosophy. They are a far greater inheritance than any amount of gold.

Introduction

On May 29th 1936, at the age of 27, Lloyd Hunnicutt graduated
from Cavalry School in Fort Riley, Kansas, as a Second Lieutenant
in the 124th Unit of the Texas National Guard. Four months later,
he eloped with his sweetheart of two years, Virginia Dickerson.
They married for a second time, at the insistence of his mother, on
January 1, 1937 at First Methodist Church in Fort Worth. So
began my father's military career and my parents' marriage.

With the words, "Know ye, that reposing special trust and
confidence in the patriotism, valor, fidelity and abilities of Sam
Lloyd Hunnicutt, I do appoint him Captain of the Cavalry in
the National Guard in the Army of the United States," my father
received his first promotion on November 18, 1940. Nineteen
months later, he went to war in the South Pacific with the
112th Cavalry.

The letters you are about to read cover the two years he
spent overseas, the first on the island of New Caledonia, which
was beautiful, non-malarial and relatively safe. The second year

was spent in New Guinea, an island of dense, humid jungle rife with malaria, where the soldiers were constantly bombarded by the Japanese.

Through these letters Lloyd sent a beam of love and humour across the Pacific Ocean to Texas. He hoped that he could take his wife with him on this unsettling adventure by means of his almost daily correspondence, which contains over 370,000 words in its original form. Due to military regulations, all soldiers had to destroy their correspondence within days of receiving it, for fear that the letters might fall into enemy hands. As a result, we can only imagine Virginia's replies.

My father returned home as a Major in July 1944. Upon returning to civilian life a few years later, he rejoined the US Army Reserves and was a full Colonel and Commandant of the 4159th Reserve Forces School upon retirement. In 1987, at the age of 78, Colonel S. L. Hunnicutt received a Special Commendation from President Reagan for services to his country.

Captain Lloyd Hunnicutt with Virginia. They are flanked by Lloyd's two orderlies, Kessler and Konkle, who were to accompany him overseas. Both "the boys" admired and respected my mother, who always treated them as part of the family.

The Letters — 1942

July 8, 1942

Everything OK. Having fine trip. No new rumors. Just passed Palm Springs – no Rita Hayworth!! Have applied for refund on fare as a result. I hated badly to leave you with all the stuff to move but can't believe Menard won't give you ample help. Have had more than enough sleep and am ready for anything that comes. Konkle and Kessler [his orderlies] join me in sending their love.

July 12, 1942, Camp Stoneman, San Francisco

I was too tired to feel like writing last night and I may be too busy later on today so I'm sending you a short note before breakfast. As you know, anything I do before breakfast is either absolutely necessary or else it is prompted by an almost superhuman urge so you should really appreciate every word that I write.

The trip was quite uneventful – everything went without a hitch. The 2nd squadron had several glasses broken out of car windows and one vestibule door was missing entirely when they arrived. They loaded their barracks bags in a baggage car then failed to be sure the car was on their train so they got here with an empty car and have not been able to locate the other baggage car at all – that makes 450 soldiers with only what they wore out here for equipment. Some fun!!

I guess my interest in trains is paying off as I don't believe anything like that could happen to me.

The boys just came in to clean my room and send their love. They don't express it just that way but that is what they mean.

We have wooden barracks and I find them very comfortable since it is relatively cool here. Not too cool for cotton but just about right all day long. It is a lovely climate and I'd like to stay here for the rest of the war.

Each officer and soldier gets a 24-hour leave for San Francisco by rotation during the coming week and I'll probably go Friday if we are still here then.

I'm letting Pearce and Rowland go today at noon and then have them back by breakfast tomorrow as they are on edge to go and Tipton, Brewton and I are able to restrain ourselves to a certain extent.

All I know about Los Angles, Fresno, etc. is that railroad yards are dirty railroad yards no matter what town they are located in. We were pulled by a varied assortment of engines including a hind-part-before one with the cab in front and I rode them all. The room is full of people and I'll just close by saying I love you until I can get some peace and quiet later.

July 17, 1942, Camp Stoneman, San Francisco
This will have to be snappy as I just finished lunch and have to fall out at 1 p.m. Incidentally, our meals are 75¢ daily cash in advance and are not fit to eat – except for bread and butter and sweet milk which we are served at breakfast.

Hazel will be thrilled to hear that I have finally seen some scenery and some sights that have amazed me. Bill and I have exactly the same ideas and have stayed together. Had a room at the Mark Hopkins on the peak of Nob Hill with a wonderful view of the harbor and within 30 minutes of arrival Bill and I were on a battleship being personally conducted by an ensign from stem to stern and bottom to top – and, by top, I mean right on up the fighting mast. Well to sum it all up, when we left yesterday we had been all over one battleship and had walked all around two others close enough to touch them and had been aboard a destroyer and a sea-going machine shop for making naval repairs.

Biggest secret of all was that the Queen Mary is in port and we got a thorough look at her. Of course, the name has been removed but I still found out. Bigger than any of the battleships by at least twice in height and about 40% longer, I judge. A really beautiful sight. All seagoing, government operated ships are painted an azure blue and it certainly makes them look pretty.

The neatest ship we saw was a Swedish medium liner which had not been painted up and was only marked by their national colors striped vertically on the hull (blue, white and gold as I recall). The rails were still in natural colors, and all the brass polished. A gorgeous sight if I ever saw one.

I can't begin to list what we saw and did. Went to Telegraph Hill and up Coit Memorial Tower. That is the point from which they used to signal ships in the old days before radio. Sort of a last message proposition. Quite interesting to us, no fooling.

I have to go now and will write another letter tonight.

I was very agreeably surprised at finding Bill to be such a good companion. He drank very little, which suited me to perfection as you know. The two of us ended up at Forbidden City Tuesday night. That is a gorgeous Chinese nightclub using all Chinese talent – and there wasn't even a cover charge.

Everyone out here knows what it means when they see officers without identification on their uniform and they are awfully nice to you. Several fellows invited us to their tables and let us dance a few dances with their dates. It was friendly of them, but I don't care to dance with anyone but you. I love you.

July 17, 1942 – Friday, Camp Stoneman
It's peaceful and quiet around here this evening, so maybe I can get a letter off that has not suffered from constant interruption.

The folks sent the pictures they took the day we left and I would like some for the boys. The one of the four of us is the best picture of you I have ever seen and I am putting it in my billfold as it is just the way I want to remember you until I get back. The boys especially want a copy apiece.

Speaking of remembering you – I think now is the time to tell you that I want you to keep buying yourself clothes and "hair-dos", etc., while I am gone as I am just going to war so I can come home to a second honeymoon and I don't want to take any old woman with me when I go on it. I really mean I want you to stay on the beam – but don't be practising on any other guys!! Platonic friendships are wonderful – except in our family.

I have been planning to phone you before I leave but I don't much think I will now. I guess I just haven't the courage. And I can't think of anything to say. This is so terribly final, somehow, that it is beyond words for me to describe my feelings. Telephoning would be sort of like taking the tourniquet off a bleeding wound just after you got it stopped a little bit.

This place is particularly rumor-free. It is so obvious that no information is going to be put out that everyone has even quit guessing where we are going from here because nobody will waste their time listening to you.

I had hoped to go to San Francisco again as I really only worked up a sightseer's appetite this trip. However, all passes cease Saturday night at midnight and I'm stuck here for any remaining time that we have. We are going on a very well known ship and have every reason to expect a happy, comfortable and safe voyage which I feel sure you will be glad to know. It is a converted passenger liner and still has the same chef that it carried before the war.

We put on a final review today for the CO of the port, a brigadier general, and he was more than pleased. We've certainly shown up the other troops in this area and the colonel is awfully well pleased about everything so far.

I hope you have accustomed yourself to life in Fort Worth by now and are enjoying yourself as much as possible. As I see it, it is vital that you keep calm and happy so our baby will have a chance to get off to a good start in life.

I never have been able to realize how things really are and it feels as if the whole war will be over soon. I guess that is nature's way of protecting us from our own thoughts.

I have to scram now and make some final property issues. I've decided to telephone you tonight but you don't know it so I have a secret from you until then. I love you.

July 19, 1942 – Sunday, Camp Stoneman
I called you this morning against my better judgment but somehow I couldn't leave without having done all that was possible to maintain our contact with each other. I'm sorry to have distressed you so much and feel that you might have been happier if I hadn't called at all. I felt pretty tough myself after you hung up, but I'm trying to do my part as well as I can.

I had a letter from you as soon as I got back to the troop and it took all day to realize you were not just across the parade ground from me. In fact, it feels silly to be writing now because you seem so near to me.

I've tried to give you a "play-by-play" report of everything I've done since I left Fort Clark and will try to keep on doing so. It's the only way I can take you with me as I go – the only way I can share my experiences with you. And I know that I will have lost the continuity of the thing by the time I get home. I don't know how much I can write and how much will be censored but I hope I can carry you with me all the way by mail. I get a tremendous kick out of writing to you. It feels almost as though I were actually talking to you instead of just making marks on paper.

There was pitifully little to be said on the telephone. Just "how are you?" and that sort of thing. But it will go with me everywhere I go – the memory of your voice and the realization of how much you love me.

Somehow, we haven't learned too well from our past separations the lessons that we should have learned. If we are ever together again, we must always remember that there are to be no unkind words, thoughts or gestures.

This is the last letter I will write for some time and I regret that there are no magic phrases that can reassure you about my going. I don't want you to worry. I want you to be calm and happy for our baby-to-be if not for yourself. And don't doubt for a moment that I want a baby because I do want one very much indeed. It is just that I love you to such an extent that I can't transfer any of my affections until the time comes.

I'm going to close now. There's no point in further elaboration because the phrase "I love you" should cover everything if you believe in me as I do in you. Certainly, I couldn't say more than that if I wrote a book. I love you.

July 30, 1942 – at sea

I must admit that I am in love with the sea and have not had even the remotest feeling of seasickness. Except for the occasional feeling of hurt when it occurs to me that I am losing my home and wife for an extended period, this has been the most interesting and enjoyable time I have ever had. I like ships and the water as you know and have, of course, investigated the ship from stem to stern and top to bottom. I am a past master of nautical phraseology and, since I am senior Officer on Duty for the voyage, I will probably have ample opportunity to increase my nautical knowledge and vocabulary considerably before we see land again. As OD – I alternate with Bill Shaw every 24 hours – I have full access to the entire ship and when I take all the dope I gather during the day and get my little map posted up every night I become very popular at least until everyone finds out where we are.

Everything has come out just as I told you in my letters before I sailed – General Johnson was either a good guesser or was remarkably well informed as his predictions at the train were quite accurate. If you'd like to know where we are in our voyage at the moment I will come as near to telling you as censorship will allow. We are at sea on an unnamed ship, traveling in an unknown direction to an unknown destination. Among the others aboard are an unknown number of people of unknown rank some of whom it is believed are members of the military service of a prominent North American country. This could go on forever, barring submarines, so I'll change the subject – but you can see that I am somewhat limited as to what I can say.

I weighed myself when I came aboard on the ship's hospital scales and weighed the old standard 162 pounds. I weighed last night on the same scales and have gone up to 175 so you will know that this is definitely a rest period for me. And I am really taking advantage of it. After all, there is a limit to the things that can be done on shipboard and, since we are constantly blacked out at night, there is ample opportunity for plenty of sleep.

We have a very nice lounge where everyone hangs out after the blackout starts at night but it gets awfully hot with the windows closed and most of us either go on deck for the evening (no cigarets) or else go to bed. I usually go to bed on alternate nights when I am not OD. There is quite a lot that goes on that I think it would be alright to tell but I'd rather not take any chances – and, of course, there has to be something left to talk about when the war is over.

If you could see me at the moment you would think I had gone nuts as I am sitting in an upper bunk leaning against the wall with my legs hanging off and the typewriter in my lap just pounding hell out of it. Somewhat inconvenient, don't you know, but it does give me the comparative peace and quiet of my cabin and the light over my left shoulder from the window. (Only the most exclusive cabins have windows, the balance having only round portholes — some fun!!)

Inasmuch as the Equator extends entirely around the world for nearly 30,000 miles, I don't suppose that it would be divulging a military secret if I told you that we were within 5 degrees of it and will cross it in the near future. We have some festivities planned: each man will get a mimeographed certificate that he can send home to his family and I understand that each officer will get a regular engraved membership in King Neptune's most exclusive club – the same type certificate that the passengers get normally. I can't get awfully enthused though as I am primarily intent on getting to where I am going and trying to whip the Japs and start back home. I'm going to be a fighting so-and-so primarily because the war is causing me the unhappiness of being separated from you – and I don't ever intend to let anything separate us again.

Don't forget what I told you about trying to enjoy yourself and buy yourself some clothes, etc. I realize that you would be awfully foolish to buy clothes right now but there is no reason why you should not really doll up after you get your figure back to normal. At the moment I feel like one child will do me for some time and the clothes you buy now won't be much good to you in a few months. I don't think we should have any more children until I get back home as I like to help decide such matters whenever it is practical and help to facilitate them.

Call the folks and tell them that I feel like a million dollars and am having the pleasantest time that I have ever had in my life as far as travelling goes. I won't write them now, as I am completely out of the letter-writing mood and have been since I left. But I'll write them after I land and have a little more to tell.

Let me hear from you soon, Virginia, because I go to sleep at night thinking of you and missing you so very much. I love you.

August 4 – Tuesday, at sea

As tomorrow is our last day to be able to get our mail into sacks, I thought I'd drop you a short note even though we are so limited in what we can write about.

Of course, the longer this voyage continues the nearer we get to the more dangerous areas and the more a sort of tension sets in among those aboard who are intelligent enough to be afraid. Not being cursed with a super abundance of intelligence, I am still enjoying the voyage to the fullest in every respect.

I am willing to admit that the ocean upon which we are traveling is a very large body of water and we are about as significant upon its surface as a flyspeck on the kitchen ceiling – and I hope we are as hard to find.

Actually as you look around you and realize that you can see water for 50 miles from horizon to horizon you do become a little awed by its magnificence. And the wake of the ship becomes a thin scar cut across its surface which heals behind you before you get out of sight of it. We hope that the aforementioned scar will not get infected by submarines.

However, we have prepared for attack from any source and I suppose most of us will be a little disappointed if nothing happens at all. Personally, I feel just like a high school girl on her first date – I want something exciting to happen but I want to be sure I can keep it under control.

I love you very much and my only regret about the whole thing is that I have to be separated from you. You are my entire pleasure in life and everything I do is for you or because of you.

Write me soon. I love you.

August 12, 1942 – New Caledonia
I'm writing for the first time since landing in New Caledonia and that is about all I can tell you. It is a lovely country so far as I can see and I am sure that our stay will be as pleasant as any stay could be away from home. We are camped on a lovely, well-drained hillside and there is plenty of cover from the sun as well as for reasonable protection from observation. It is very much like any other of the places we have ever camped except Fort Bliss which this has beaten at least a hundred ways. There is plenty of good grass to sleep on and the climate is delightful, even though

this is the cold, rainy season. We can work all day in cotton clothing without being uncomfortable – and there are lovely beaches nearby where we can swim as we did today. Of course, they are reported to be teeming with tiger sharks but that doesn't scare us anymore than the Japs. So far the food has been delicious and three natives drove a good-looking herd of fat steers through our area today so I am inclined to think we may get a little fresh beef from time to time. We have lots of dehydrated foods, and they appear highly satisfactory. Had dried cabbage and dried potatoes and the flavor absolutely unimpaired.

I have not seen a white person outside of Army and Navy personnel since I landed and it is obvious that intercourse (social and otherwise) is out for the Gay Lotharios. The native women sit around on their haunches chewing on a snuff stick. All the natives seem to be of very happy and friendly natures and I am sure that the fact that they speak no English (this is a French possession) is one of the reasons they seem to be less intelligent.

Virginia, I know my letters have been somewhat impersonal but it has helped me stall off that inevitable realization of the 7,000 miles between us not to put my thoughts of you and my loneliness for you on paper. I steel myself constantly against thinking how wide that ocean is and how hopelessly far we are apart. If I could walk home at 20 miles per day, it would take me exactly a year to get there. Sweetheart, that is a long, long way. But I'd start walking it tonight if I knew I could spend just 24 hours with you when I get there. It's a little hard for me to try to tell you how I feel. The things I told you while we were on maneuvers were about as expressive as I know how to be – and they would sound so inadequate as to be silly now!! Unusual for me to lack the words, I know! But it's true, nevertheless.

And I'm not at all unmindful of your condition. I worry about you constantly and hope that you are past the "morning sickness" stage and able to enjoy yourself a little more. I'm sure that I am much happier than you in many ways and I regret that I can't assume some of your burden as I believe I could if I were there with you. I think I have probably come nearer to being a good husband to you when you were sick than at any other time and I believe I could help you a lot if it were possible.

It seems funny to think that I will come home to a child who will have been born almost without my knowledge. But I know that I will be crazy about it although my major concern now is the fear that something might happen to you – I don't believe I could ever get over that.

I hope you will let everyone be kind to you as I know both our families are so anxious to be. I insist on your being very, very careful so that nothing can happen to you or our baby. I love you. (You will probably get this before you get my ship orders.)

August 17, 1942 – Monday, New Caledonia
The island is really very nice. We have an irrigation ditch running through our camp that is full of fresh mountain water. Our drinking water comes from a city (ha! ha!) main but we use the local water for coffee, cooking, washing and bathing. We have everything for maintenance of life but nothing to help us enjoy it. There is no refreshment available in town except ice cream or milk shakes made of goat's milk (you can imagine my reaction to that). I've been to town once to collect the troop payroll and was able to buy a can of Nestles Dried Whole Milk to mix with water for my breakfast food and we consider that quite a luxury. It cost 20 francs (there are 43 per $1 American) and that is a little steep as it was not a large can at all.

We completed a luxurious 2-holer today that I find very pleasant. It almost makes me homesick for my childhood built as it is in the Early American tradition. No doubt but that there is where I'll spend my happiest hours lost in meditation.

Unfortunately there is no printed matter of any sort available so far as I can find anywhere on the island. I read the directions on canned goods that we get several times per day in order not to lose the art entirely. I am even tempted at times to read the daily bulletin!!

We received a free issue of about a carton of cigarets per man yesterday including a box of 50 cigars and 56 plugs of chewing tobacco and It was greatly appreciated. However, the nicest thing happened when we passed out a little ditty bag to each man that contained a deck of cards, a little sewing kit, a 25¢ novel (like I used to read) and other odds and ends. Most of them had the names of the donors in them (they came through the Red Cross) and some had letters of good wishes. It was really touching to see how some of these big ugly guys looked as they went through them and realized that somewhere somebody had a kind thought for them. It really is pretty tough to be 7,000 or 8,000 miles from home and to have no amusements, no shows, no beer or liquor and no woman around of any description.

I seem to have become very much of a philosopher and take things as they come. I get pleasure out of the simplest things – a good bath or a hearty meal is to be treated reverently. I miss not having you in the room when I read and not having you to come home to when I finish my day's work. I really can't express it but maybe you will understand. We share so much besides our physical attraction for each other that the physical is minimized tremendously when we are separated. When I feel a sudden pang of loneliness for you it's because I miss the sight of you and the sound of you and the feeling that you are nearby when I need you the most, and how much I love you.

August 18, 1942 – V-Mail

This is something new and I'll try anything once – so here goes. I had my first shower in New Caledonia this afternoon. There is an irrigation ditch running through our camp and a steep slope on one side of it. I conceived the idea of cutting bamboo (it grows to be 40 feet tall and 5 to 6 inches in diameter) and piping the water out to a point where it is over our heads, then hanging a bucket over the end of it with the bottom full of nail holes. The whole troop gathered around while I took the first

"V-Mails". These one-page letters, much disliked by Lloyd, became necessary as the war lengthened and the volume of post increased.

Scenes from New
Caledonia including
(below) the "bamboo
cane and bucket with
nail holes" shower
proudly rigged up by
Lloyd.

ABOVE: Kessler
holding a splendid bunch
of bananas brought back
to camp by Lloyd.

shower and it was plenty cold – but it was unusually refreshing and I feel swell.

We are averaging ten to eleven hours of sleep per night as it is impossible to use lights after dark and there's nothing else to do after 6:30 in the evening. We are getting as comfortable as possible under the circumstances and I am still eating prodigious meals.

Give the family my love and tell them that I'll write as often as possible. I haven't been able to receive any mail as yet and it seems awfully lonesome at the moment. I love you.

August 24, 1942 – V-Mail

A good old-fashioned siege of homesickness wouldn't be so bad – but these constantly recurring twinges of emptiness that occur when something unconsciously reminds me of you are a little hard to take. I don't see now how I even had the nerve to get on the train at Fort Clark. I know now why American soldiers always win their battles – they fight hard so they can get home to their wives and families. I think our greatest hardship is that there is no one near who loves us and to whom we can turn for comfort. Each of us must stand on his own feet at all times. But that is enough of that. Remember that without your love I would have no incentive for anything ever again.

September 2, 1942

I'll try to answer as many of your questions as I can. You see, officers are pretty much their own censors although they occasionally censor some of our mail when it reaches the mainland. Since it is left to me to censor my own mail, I am probably a little more careful than I would be otherwise. I really appreciate being able to write you without some stranger reading my most personal and intimate thoughts, therefore I don't want to take advantage of the privilege.

The nearest town is very nice to look at but is deserted when we go in. All the stores close on Wednesday and Saturday afternoons and the natives (whites, I mean) disappear so there is no opportunity of getting acquainted. I've been in three times but two of the trips were on business and I didn't get to see a lot – the governor's house and Army headquarters and a few things like that. Of course, loving ships like I do, I enjoyed visiting the docks for a few minutes and I did get a good meal on each of my last two trips.

I turned the troop over to Jack yesterday and am now Rupe's executive officer. I'm expecting to do some plain and fancy relaxing. Of course, I attend drill and all that but I don't have to feed, house, clothe, supply and father 150 men any more. In regard to promotions, Lt. Col. Miller will probably have a "corner" on his rank in this outfit for some time. Rupe has the squadron and I honestly wouldn't swap with him for a thousand dollars flat. You can't imagine the sweet relief that I have. The Colonel is on his tail continually and I just stand back, listen and say, "But for the grace of God—".

As to our life here, I can't go into any detail, but if you can imagine Fort Clark without any homes, or barracks, or picture shows, or beer, Cokes, liquor, ice, or anything else of comfort to the human body, then you have a play-by-play description. The only exceptions I can think of are that the drill ground is considerably rougher and the toilets get filled up instead of stopped up.

As to reading matter, we only have what we brought on the boat and that is gradually getting out of date. The chaplain has a small library but I haven't been over it as yet, and don't know what books he has or how good they are. I expect to have more time to read now, though, and will see how they go in a day or two.

I really feel like a "heller" tonight. It's nine o'clock and I opened a brand new Hershey bar to celebrate my first letter. I guess it sounds a little silly for a grown man to admit but I "clouded up and rained" a little when I started to read it and realized so keenly that you were real and alive and in love with me and were waiting for me to come home to you. Sometimes it seems as though our life together was something to be looked back upon as a wonderful memory like childhood rather than something that has just suffered an interruption and can be recommenced later on. I truly do not believe that a million dollars could have made me any happier than those six pages from you.

Don't worry too much about my boredom. I can stand a lot of solitude without hurting. What I miss most is the feeling of having you near me. Of walking in the front door and knowing that you are there waiting for me. You remember how mad I used to get when you would be next door or playing bridge? Just selfishness, I know. But, hell, if you can't be selfish of your wife, what is there that you can be selfish of?

I hear everyone coming back from a picture show that they walked a mile to two to see. Poor devils, not everyone could have as sweet a letter to answer tonight as I have.

Remember that you are not to worry about me at all. I'm fine and dandy. You just keep the baby factory going and don't be flaunting your newly acquired curves for the benefit of the slackers. I love you.

September 3, 1942

I wrote you at length last night but will send you this note because I became a major this afternoon and, of course, want you to know first. Quite a few of the fellows at headquarters haven't heard from home yet including the colonel and I suppose it is because their mail is not being sent air mail. If you happen to contact any of the Dallas girls, you might tell them about it. Ordinary mail is awfully slow.

I got home too late to go to the creek for a cold shower as it chills you to the bone after dark. I have both feet in a bucket of icy water now letting them soak as we march quite a little and it seems to toughen them up.

Write me often, Virginia, as letters are terribly important to my happiness here and I need all you can possibly send. I love you.

September 7, 1942

I'm doing as much reading as possible in order to pass the time. My reading is really a lifesaver because I feel more at home with a book than I ever feel otherwise. Not a great selection though to choose from.

I bought some maple-leaf insignia on the boat coming over and it was a good thing as there are none available here at all. I have one pair and if I lose one it will be just too bad. Being a major is very nice so far although I haven't paid a great deal of attention to it. Our pay will now be as follows:

Base pay	$250.00
Longevity	$25.00 (after Nov. – $12.50 now)
Overseas pay	$25.00
Subsistence	$63.00
Rental	<u>$105.00</u>
	$468.00

After our allotment gets straightened, I will allot all I am allowed and keep the rental only which will be $350.50 for you at the start and $363.00 later on. I hope we can save $250.00 per month while I am here. That will help a little to salve my pain at our undoubtedly long separation. That would give us $3,000.00 per year in the sock and I'm willing to scrimp for it if you are. As soon as I get about $100.00 ahead for emergencies, I should be able to send at least $48.00 per month home out of my share.

There is an army program on the scout-car radio tonight. A bunch of patriotic hooey that we care nothing about. What we need is Jack Benny or Fred Allen or some good dance music. You can pretty well take a man's patriotism for granted when he is seven or eight thousand miles from home with his gun loaded and aching to fight. You certainly don't need to hand him any bunch of morale baloney. All these boys want is a whack at the Japs so they can get this war over and come home. Me too! Tell our folks hello for me. I love you.

September 17, 1942

I intend to keep myself busy as some of the guys who stay here awhile get a little screw loose. I hear quite a few tales about the pyschopathics from Pearce and Thomas who have occasional business at the hospital. Not that I'm the type to go psychopathic at all but I do think that keeping busy is a big help toward keeping happy. Otherwise I get that lost feeling like you are afraid of something and don't really know what it is. But I do know. I'm afraid of being away from you for a long, long time. I love you.

September 18, 1942

Got a letter from you and one from Mama which makes 5 letters in 2 days. I wrote you about the other 3 last night so I'll not go into details again. Let it suffice to say that I am probably the happiest man in camp by a least a 3-to-1 margin at the moment.

In order to really celebrate I lit two candles at the same time to read them and am drinking my last can of grape juice even though there is no more available anywhere on the whole island.

I want you to be extremely careful and not run any chance of hurting yourself by too much activity until you are able after the baby is born. Having babies is a very important business but it is definitely secondary to your health and well being to me. I married you because I love you and want to live with you until I am an old, old man regardless of the number of children we may have, if any. Don't for a moment ever forget that no matter what happens, you are my whole life and don't ever think differently.

Don't be misled about the radios we are issued. The regiment has drawn one radio to date and that is installed in the colonel's tent so you can count the number of times the rest of us have used it on the fingers of Venus de Milo's left hand! I love you.

September 22, 1942

I read the Bible quite a lot, especially the New Testament and get more pleasure from it than you would suspect. However I am not becoming religious, so don't be alarmed. I don't have a great deal else to read and find it more interesting than I had remembered. It is easy to profit from the Bible whether you are religious or not and is an excellent guide from the common sense point of view. I especially like to read those parts that touch on love and marriage because they make me think of you and our life together.

I'm learning to correct a lot of mistakes that I've been making for years. I eat breakfast every morning although most consist of coffee and a couple of individual boxes of dry cereal with sugar and milk. If dinner and/or supper are unpalatable (that means if we have canned meat), I fill up on bread and jelly and never let a meal past without eating a reasonable amount of food. And, more important, I relax and get some sleep at night so that I am able to do much more in less time and with less worry than I've ever been able to do before.

And I am learning the value of simple everyday things. For instance, Hooks and I found an orange tree the other day on reconnaissance and we swore each other to secrecy as to its location. We go up and gather the riper ones once a week and pass them around. They are so much more important here than they would be at home where you can get all you want instead of walking several miles and hunting for them as we do here.

I imagine having a baby will simplify our life quite a little. I'm sure that taking care of it will be quite a task for you. I don't want it to be such a burden that it will turn us into "old folks", though. For one thing, that wouldn't be fair to the child. I don't ever want a child of mine to be afraid of me or think I am narrow minded. And I want it to be reared in a happy home where there is no fussing and a minimum of unpleasantness. Of course, I know you feel the same way and I don't know why I write all this – except I want to share in the baby some way and that's pretty hard to do "from here, doctor".

If we're not careful, we're apt to build up such an idyllic conception of our marriage that we'll be dissatisfied with our mere mortal efforts to make it come true after the war is over. Of course, I'm joking. I love you.

September 29, 1942

The colonel has gotten some native soldiers to build a fairly large sized assembly hall for the officers and ordered a dance for Saturday night for which each of us anted up $5.00. It's bound to be a "rat race" for sure as I can't believe they could dig up 10 women on the entire island and we have nearly 80 of us in addition to the invitation list which he has graciously offered to take off our hands and handle by himself. That means a bunch of hot shots will be here and our boys will probably be roped off in a corner away from the girls entirely.

If the thing pleases him, the investment will be worthwhile and I don't care about the female phase of it. However, it is a little hard on our lieutenants to have no access to any sort of transportation when the boys from other units jeep up to the nurses' quarters in GI vehicles and carry off the cream of the crop.

I still don't anticipate our getting into anything. The views I had at Fort Clark about our chance of combat have been strengthened since I arrived here and you are not to worry about us. If I become a casualty it will be from rolling out of bed.

The reason that I have a few moments to spare is that we are preparing to put on a review for some visiting firemen. This one is a little more worthwhile than usual though I think I'd best not mention for whom it is being given. There is little question but that we put on an outstanding parade as we are selected for every visitor apparently without exception. In fact, Major Tracy told me when I visited him recently that they still sing our praises at Stoneman as the fanciest outfit that has been shipped out from there since the camp was built. And that's no faint praise from a former member of the 1st Cavalry Division staff who graduated from West Point.

Write to me as often as you feel like it and remember that I am all yours and no substitutes. I love you.

October 2, 1942

I went to the picture show last night and arrived a little late. Sat on the edge of the crowd down fairly close to the front. It was an awfully dark and cloudy night and a high wind blew the screen (2 sheets patched together) down twice almost before it started. I don't know how to describe it except to say that it was a "nervous" night with the darkness and the eeriness of the hard wind. Anyhow, in the middle of the show, I suddenly found I was being trampled by the whole goddam regiment, or so it seemed at the time. I finally managed to get on my feet but I had been stepped on considerably and my knee was sprained a little. I went back as the panic died down and found two or three men hurt. Petrie was out cold and apparently had a few injuries although not serious. They haled him off on a stretcher and we settled back to see the rest of the show.

Here is what had happened. The guard tent was toward the back of where we were all seated and a member of the guard was cleaning his gun. When he finished he put it back in the holster and it went off, shooting the bottom out of the holster and hitting him in the leg.

The outdoor speakers with the projector are pretty loud and I was sitting near one and didn't even hear the shot and apparently no else paid any attention to it. The corporal of the guard or someone got the ambulance and the boy was put into it at the top of the hill behind the crowd. Then the driver, who had his lights turned off to keep from ruining the picture, started down the hill along the edge of the crowd opposite the side I was on and someone walked in front of him so that he didn't run over anyone.

Apparently some guy who had been absorbed in the picture looked up and saw it rolling quietly down the hill and thought it was running away and hollered, causing the sudden wave of mass hysteria that resulted. It was really an amazing thing and made quite an impression on me although I can't really describe it to you. (I suppose it would be an anticlimax to tell you that the pictures were Victor McLaglen and Sally Eilers in *Full Confession* (lousy) and Abbott and Costello in *Rio Rita* (pretty good).)

I haven't gotten any more stamps and I'm borrowing one for this letter. I guess I write too often but it's the only real pleasure I have and six cents every day or two should not be too expensive. So, please shoot me some stamps often as I can't get any here at all. I'd like to have a camera and about 12 rolls of film and enough developing paper to develop them on. I can get the work done here but they have no supplies and no cameras or film available. Just call it my Christmas present. I love you.

October 4, 1942

The colonel had his party last night and everyone seemed to have had a good time and so did I. There were about 125 officers and a few civilians (French), 20 nurses and about 10 French women from downtown most of whom came with their husbands who were either French officers or island officials. Everything was quite gay and lots of effort had been put into the thing. The nurses were mostly from a nearby hospital but some came all the way from a hospital about 60 miles away. They are a pretty independent bunch and it was kind of funny to watch some of our better known woman-chasers following them around and getting no place at all.

One officer who speaks no French was heard trying to get a Frenchman who spoke no English to proposition a French girl for him. Unfortunately, it was the Frenchman's wife! Anyhow, that's the story that was being told at the table today at noon.

I've spent most of today fixing up a place to re-pitch my tent. I have been able to get some boards 12" wide and am making a box the size of the bottom of my tent like a sandbox over which I am going to pitch the tent. This will make the walls about a foot higher and keep me from having to stoop over every time I turn around. I'm covering the floor with clay and tamping it. I'd like to find a woven bamboo or reed mat to cover it with but the only one I've seen was $9 and I don't need it that badly. I'm really very comfortable and am mostly fixing it up so I'll be ready for the rainy season when it arrives. We've been having light showers regularly but I understand that it will really cut loose in another month or so.

I think about you constantly. I love you.

October 12, 1942

I suppose that today has been the most heartbreaking day I've spent in a long time. The colonel was gone all day and I went into town and spent the afternoon trying to buy you something for Christmas and couldn't find anything at all. I went to every store in town and there was literally nothing there.

It's really pitiful to see that there is store after store with their shelves absolutely empty. Apparently nothing comes through except a little foodstuff from Australia – canned corned beef, canned tongue, canned mackerel, etc. We do buy ourselves a little canned butter from time to time and I found a store today that would sell me a couple of bottles of Lea & Perrins.

I tried to buy cloth to make three or four pillowslips for my little bedroll pillow that is only 10 x 14 inches and couldn't find any anywhere. I sure hate it that I couldn't get anything at all worth sending but I just couldn't.

We had a part of a picture show the other night. Irene Dunne and Douglas Fairbanks, Jr. in *The Joy of Living,* but the generator burned out in the middle of it and everybody stood up and cheered when they announced that it couldn't be finished.

I'm becoming more attached to my horse every day, but I think it's too bad that horses are not good for anything except as pets any more. I don't know why they keep cavalry at all and wonder at it more every day. We could go ahead without them if they ever needed us badly enough. It would make our time spent in horse training pretty much a waste though.

MInd you, all the time I spend away from you seems pretty much a waste. It must be because I love you.

October 16, 1942

There is some talk of calling off our dance tomorrow night and that suits me fine. I've felt that they were a little unsuitable all along although many of the officers do seem to get a "lift" out of them. But I've been to the hospital a couple of times and I can't help but feel we should work as hard as we can and rest when we're not working. I can't seem to forget that, within a few hours' flight from here, soldiers as good and clean and fine as ours are being put through living hell.

My horse has turned out to be the pet of the squadron. However, he piled me up yesterday in the fullest sense of the word and no fooling. It was my own fault though so I can't complain. I was jumping him for the first time and he was, as a result, unusually nervous. I stopped to watch some troopers jumping and turned loose the reins so he could eat. Then I decided to dismount and made the mistake of raking my heel across his rump and he started pitching. I was ready to step to the ground and should have done so but, for some reason or other, I tried to straddle him again. It definitely didn't work out and I lit fair flat on my fanny. Didn't do any serious damage although I'm somewhat sore all over. I'll not make that mistake again!!

Currency issued by the Bank of Indo-China — souvenirs from New Caledonia.

I am wrapping you a very small and insignificant package that you don't need to hold off opening till Christmas. A couple of things I got a French woman to make downtown when I walked my feet off trying to find something suitable. The little handkerchiefs don't amount to much but, at least, they prove I was thinking of you.

We were seated at the table today at noon and Tascarella was dwelling on what we'd all do when we got back to SF He predicted that one person would end up in bed with a blonde; another, a brunette; another would spend his first night drinking, etc. He skipped me entirely and when someone asked him what he thought I'd be doing, he said, "Aw, hell, he'll be at the telephone office calling his wife!" And I will be. I love you.

October 23, 1942

I never go into details as to how I miss you at times as I used to do on maneuvers. After all I could feel sure that I'd be home to satisfy my longings for you in a few weeks at the most.

I think the reason that my desires are so truly for you alone is that I don't have to resort to my imagination to visualize what I want so badly. I merely have to relax and allow my memory to go to work in order to spend the most painfully sweet hours that I have ever spent. And I do mean painfully sweet!

And my memory is so very, very dependable. I honestly believe that I will have remembered at least once before I come home every little intimacy that we have ever shared. Of course, the nature of my desires hasn't changed since we've been married or since I've been away, but my thoughts cling to the tangible memory of you and your every little gesture and movement like a drowning person clings to their savior and I don't believe that my mind could ever turn loose of that to grasp for anything less tangible such as an ordinary desire for sexual satisfaction from just any woman.

I have always been afraid that, should we ever be separated indefinitely, I might revert to my old ways and I've spent lots of time trying to understand why I haven't. I believe I know and I'm sure you'll understand from what I've said. You remember that I've often said while you were in my arms that having anyone else would be an anticlimax. That could have been brought on

by the ecstasies of the moment. But there are no ecstasies to
this moment and I still feel the same way.

If I knew that I'd never make love to you again so long as I
lived, I'd still want to come home and share my life with you
before I'd accept anyone else. It must be because I love you.

October 24, 1942

You used to complain that I wouldn't tell you I loved you often
enough but I don't think you have been able to make that
complaint for a long, long time. For I've devoted the last
several years to proving to you that I loved you alone and
wanted no one else. I hope it has not been a wasted effort
because I am so anxious for you to have complete confidence
in me. I don't want your love for me to waver for a moment. I
want to come home to a second honeymoon. (We never really
had our first, did we?)

I've been through two marriage ceremonies in my life (both
with you!) and I can't think of anything sweeter than to come
home to another. Of course, it really isn't socially correct to
have your own baby at your wedding, I know. But I could go
through that ceremony with you again and again and have it
mean a little more each time. No sultan with his vast harems
ever knew more varieties of pleasures than you have given me
in the past six years. And I'm awfully glad now that I realized
what I had in you for a wife and did not wait for distance to
"lend enchantment".

I believe you know that I realized the almost phenomenal
suitability that we have for one another and I think you know that
I appreciate its value to the fullest. I haven't been writing to you
in this vein so much and I don't intend to continue with it
regularly because it is more than mildly torturous to sit and recall
the minute details of our life together now that we are so far
apart. Nevertheless, one doesn't have an anniversary every day
and I started early last night to thinking of you so vividly that it
has carried over through my dreams and into my day.

Recollections are the greatest pleasure that we have over here and I really believe that I am glad I don't have a radio most of the time. You know that I always have a tune in my head and, since I can't learn any new ones, the tunes I recall bring with them many times memories that are most pleasant. Most of the important things in my life are subconsciously connected to some particular piece of music.

You mentioned in your letter that you were reluctant to be too personal in your remarks because you hated to have them read by a stranger. You can forget that as none of your letters have ever been opened until I got them. I'm sure the mail service has all they can do reading our outgoing mail without tackling the letters coming this way – so just fire your best barrel.

I don't gloss over our occasional fusses and fights and I think that I realize our faults. In fact, I feel that our life together has been sweeter because our love has been strong enough to teach us to be tolerant of each other and to forgive each other for unpleasantnesses that have occurred from time to time. And I'm also sure that these little differences will arise from time to time in the future. But I am equally convinced that we will be able to overcome them even more easily than we ever have before.

Nothing less than war has ever separated us for any material length of time and I intend for us to never be apart again. I plan for us to subordinate everything to our life together in the future and to make a home that will be a sanctuary for us and a proper place for our child to live in.

Above all, I intend for us to keep our love and desire for each other as young and fresh and alive as it has been these past six years. It's a wonderful help to me now to know that we never missed an opportunity to have each other when it was possible for us to be together. I'd hate to sit over here and think we'd wasted a moment of our time together. And I hope you'll agree that we will never waste another.

Write me as often as you feel able but always remember that your prime job is concerned with the baby now and don't do more than you feel able to do. You must take care of yourself above everything else. Give my love to your grandmother and everyone. I love you.

October 25, 1942

I got your V-mail of 25 September yesterday and I must admit that the list of stuff you estimated there as already having been mailed to me was quite prepossessing. It is sort of silly, I guess, to hear a person say that they are anticipating the receipt of 1 can of pineapple juice. The only way for anyone at home to really understand would be for them to forego all luxuries for a few weeks and live on bread and jam, with some watery potatoes (dehydrated) and corned beef hash to break the monotony when you just can't stand bread and jam any more. And don't forget the big, golden kernels of canned corn that is fugitive from the feed box of a Missouri mule. Anyhow, the only point in the above is to tell you why I appreciate your sending me a box as I suppose now we will all live.

It appears that my missing the dances is beginning to pay dividends. Bill got a letter from Edith complaining that someone had been sending home a few choice and highly descriptive paragraphs about his life among the females of the island (I didn't get the details but I think he was supposed to have been out with a nurse or something). It is just barely possible that it could be true. I'd lay a month's salary that it is a damned lie – and I'd bet another that I know who told it.

All I've heard or seen of Bill that was out of line at all was that he has been "under the influence" a time or two. If getting drunk occasionally is a sin, then it is only the lack of drinking liquor that keeps most of us from going to hell in a hurry – and especially the guy I think wrote home about Bill. Actually, the few nurses that are available on the island get a tremendous rush and there are enough young fellows like Pearce, Rowland, Thomas and the other collegiates to keep them more than busy and the few I danced with at the first dance were quite respectful of my rank and talked to me like I'd talk to your father. And so, I just don't believe that Bill can walk in a total stranger from outpost duty and reap the harvest from the fields these boys have been cultivating so assiduously.

Anyhow, life over here is unpleasant enough without having someone start trouble between a man and his wife, especially when the wife is so far away that the man can't defend himself even if he wanted to do so. And being unhappy or worried about things at home can certainly destroy your morale and efficiency when you are living as we do.

Thinking like this makes me miss you all the more. Write to me often. I love you.

October 28, 1942

It seems funny to sit here writing this letter to you and realize that it will probably be just before Christmas when you get it. I've never thought much about it until I let our anniversary slip up on me and I couldn't get a letter to you or wire you to let you know that I remembered. It has always been so easy to communicate with each other that I only needed to think of things a few days in advance. Here if you don't think of things at least six weeks in advance it's too late. I know that we have another anniversary January 1st, but I don't know when to write to get a letter home within 10 days of it. I can't help but feel that the first one was the important one for us, anyhow. It made everything legal.

I'll be true to you forever and I'll love you as long as you will let me. I don't suppose that is a great deal but you can at least be sure it's true.

November 7, 1942

I haven't written for two or three days for two very good reasons. I've been too busy to have the time for one and I've been in a mental slump for the other. I just occasionally get awfully lonesome for you and for a little the whole thing doesn't seem worthwhile.

I don't suppose we are ever really happy over here – but most of the time it is bearable. Just every now and then I look ahead and wonder how long it will be before I can come home to you and it sort of gets me down. I have as hard a time as anyone to fight my funks because I can't turn to liquor or women or gambling to snap me out of it. And reading is a mild stimulant in itself. But I can always overcome it or, at least, I am able to file the whole thing in my "subconscious" for future reference.

It would be easier if there were more tangible obstacles to overcome. Like hurdles in a race where you were obviously making progress as you went along. But I have the occasional frustrated feeling of wanting to get ahead and waking to find my feet tied together.

When I realize the gamble that marriage is for a couple who can only imagine their future together, it almost makes me believe in companionate marriage. We could easily have turned out to be unsuited to each other and never have realized what we were missing. We would have thought of marriage as being considerably overrated and made the best of it, I suppose.

I never did get the letter about baby names and it is the only letter you have sent to date that I am sure I haven't received. I'm sorry too as I'd hate to have supported you in an unaccustomed state of extreme poverty for the past 6 years and still have a nameless child. Especially after having devoted my entire lifetime quota of marriages on you.

Write me soon and remember that I think of you constantly (and pleasantly). I love you.

November 15, 1942

We had our fourth dance last night (or fifth, I can't remember) and I went over for a change. I had to go to town yesterday afternoon in connection with some court-martial investigations (one of our boys beat the hell out of three Marine Corps MPs) and Col. Fowler and Maj. Ketts of the AA Artillery asked to bring a New Zealand colonel and a French lieutenant with them to the party. I have never enjoyed anyone so much as the Anzac colonel who has spent the last two years in Suva (Fijis). A very high type person and a most interesting conversationalist. The Australians and New Zealanders are strong for the US and I feel sure that they will be our friends for many years if not actually united to us by strong ties – at least economically.

They've been left in the lurch down here in this end of the world and no one has really come to their aid except the United States. They seem to appreciate it, too.

There was a new shipment of nurses received last week and they were invited to the dance – from Massachusetts, largely. And I do mean largely!! They are the brawniest women I've seen in a long time anywhere.

Everything has been going pretty smoothly for the past few days in the regiment and the colonel shows an occasional tendency to be human. Of course, nobody really counts on it, though. He has many fine qualities and is so highly respected as a soldier by all of us that I often regret he doesn't break down a little more and be friendlier and more trusting of us. It would at least add 25% to the morale and general efficiency of the regiment.

I'm really burning to be with you and I just want to write and write to keep you vividly before me. I knew that I didn't want to leave you to come over here – and I am even more positive that I will never leave you again after this is over.

We've been robbing ourselves for a long time in several ways. I have worked too hard and neither of us has regulated our habits properly with the result that we've not had the maximum of pleasure that we could have had. I intend to go to bed early when I come home and then have one or two good nights a week – picture shows and a dance or night club at least twice or more a month. Of course, if I get a lot of rest (and you don't go too "maternal" with the child and everything), we'll probably have to have an auxiliary bed, as one couldn't stand the punishment.

I know that if I didn't have the vivid recollections of our life together, it wouldn't be so easy for me over here. I spend every idle moment recalling the minutest details. Oddly enough, my desire for you, by being so strong, leaves little opportunity for me to desire anyone else. I just don't believe there could be anything remotely approaching our perfection without the hours we have devoted to each other and the love we share as an incentive.

I don't think it helps a great deal for us to inflame each other when we are so far apart but I just can't help it every now and then – probably because I love you.

November 20, 1942

I got up and dressed one morning and had marched the detachment to the drill field for calisthenics when an officer on the staff told me that I was to pack my bedroll and other equipment preparatory to a two or three day boat trip with a detail consisting of one lieutenant and 22 selected NCOs. (They sent non-coms because the trip offered an unusual change in our routine and the men were selected on a basis of merit and given the trip as a reward.)

Kessler started packing our stuff and I went to headquarters to get the dope and found that I was to go on what they called a "submarine reconnaissance". This consisted actually of riding about halfway around the island and looking over the shore line in order to familiarize myself with spots that might, for one reason or another, lend themselves to the landing of Jap troops or as resting and watering places for submarines.

I got the detail ready and assembled for transportation to a nearby port to embark, then issued each man a set of maps and the areas to be covered together with an idea of our mission and the type of information we were after. We arrived to find that the boat, an ex-Japanese fishing and trading vessel, would be delayed until afternoon because they were still loading fuel (diesel) oil. Also a couple of guys from the Signal Corps were installing a two-way radio for use by a later group coming into port.

This was a little annoying for an hour or so and then we became grateful for the delay as the most tremendous ship I have ever seen, an airplane carrier, came gliding by followed at regular intervals by its complement of smaller vessels: those that protect it from attack by vessels while its airplanes are away on a mission. It was a truly thrilling sight and would lift the morale of anyone who saw it just to realize that we could continue to manufacture such gigantic things almost at will. As you know, I have seen a number of battleships and they are completely dwarfed both in length and especially in height by the carrier. (I suppose this is because the flight deck is built above the ship and lends a massive appearance to its general outline.)

We finally got under way in the middle of the afternoon and everything was literally "smooth sailing" while we were still in the harbor, which is large and calm. Then we hit the open sea and the fun began.

In order to explain exactly the manner in which the ship behaved I will have to describe it a little. It was about 70 or 80 feet long and, at least to me, unusually narrow, and definitely of the "old maid" type giving an impression of skinny angularity with not a curve showing. Its later actions in high waves led me to believe it had a very round bottom, but since the water offered modest concealment, I am not in a position to say for certain.

Anyhow, after we had been out of the confines of the harbor about 30 minutes, it really began to rock and roll. We were heading directly into the waves, which I judged to be about 10 or 15 feet high (not an unusual height at all), and as the front of the ship rode up and to the top of a wave, it would stick out over the trough behind it until its weight ahead of the crest was enough to cause it to fall like a seesaw with a tremendous slap back into the water sending up barrels of water which a fairly strong wind blew all over us.

When we started out of the harbor we passed a troop transport headed in and everyone had hurried up to the front end to get a good view. I was sitting on a cross piece at the very forepeak and everyone was laughing and yelling as the ship went through its trapeze act. After about 15 minutes I looked around and found that only myself and three others were left. The others were toward the rear of the ship dangling across the lee rail tossing their cookies.

The fact that the boat had a propensity for rolling from side to side as well as from front to rear is what led me to suspect the round bottom and added nothing to the happiness of most of those aboard.

Finally those of us who were not "unwell" became hungry and sat up there in full view of everyone eating cans of meat and beans from our choice stock of Type C rations much to their displeasure and our amusement. We all deserved to be washed overboard, and couldn't have been wetter if we had been.

It got dark far too soon for me and the skipper put into a sheltered passage to spend the night because we could no longer see the shore and because we were approaching a particularly dangerous stretch of reefs which he (and I) preferred to navigate by daylight.

There were only four bunks aboard which the lieutenants, the two master sergeants and I occupied. The balance who were, at the best, somewhat damp had to sleep on the deck under the inadequate shelter of their two bed blankets. They were so thankful to be in the relatively calm harbor that I don't think they minded their cold, hard beds at all.

I hated to stop as I enjoyed everything about the trip except the constant pounding of the engine which shook the ship until you felt it would fall apart. To give you an idea of how badly it shook, I will tell you that, just for fun, a group of us laid a washer on a table and took turns trying to place our forefinger on it without having to move our finger along the surface of the table. Our average miss was approximately two inches!!

We started up again before sunup the following morning and ran until about dark that night at which time we reached our destination and landed to get a good hot meal at a native hotel. It was doubly welcome because our normal diet is nothing to brag about and because we had had nothing to eat except cold canned rations for two days.

Most of the boys enjoyed the second day very well, as it was, for the most part, relatively mild. We got in lots of good work with the maps and I taught them how to plot their position on the water by shooting compass azimuths at known points on the shore and then plotting them on the maps. Really a very simple procedure but unusual for cavalry at sea, you must admit.

We came home by truck across the island which I will save as subject for another travelogue. It was an exciting trip in itself as we had to cross the backbone of the mountains on a road that was so narrow that we had to back up two or three times to get around sharp corners and a miscue of six inches would have given us a much needed but highly undesired bath in a mountain stream a couple of hundred feet below us.

We passed quite a few native villages but the road traffic is governed by a time system to prevent meetings over its narrowest and highest portions and I was, as a consequence, afraid to stop and visit. It may be just as well as my guidebook says, "One must bear in mind that less than 100 years ago…they were still in the Stone Age… (and) they were cannibals and the bodies of their enemies killed in battle were the only meat at their disposal."

We got in at noon of the third day and were quite thankful that it was a half holiday and we could get a little rest before returning to the milder sensation of rocking and rolling on our horses. As I had to go to court the following day it meant that my horse had gone unridden for six days all of which had done nothing to the benefit of his discipline which, at the best, is never high. All in all, a great adventure and almost makes our separation bearable. Almost! I love you.

November 21, 1942

We took the first of three weekly bubonic plague shots yesterday and my left arm is a little sore although I don't feel bad otherwise at all. We had expected the "casualties" from it to deplete our ranks considerably for the review this morning but I haven't heard of but one real complaint. Before we got started this morning Rupert had to drop out. He feels better now though and was at the supper table tonight.

If I amaze you with a pedantic plethora of multi-syllabled words, just relax and remember that I have managed to acquire a Pocketbook Dictionary. It is relatively small and the definitions are clear and short. I am glad to have it as I know many words but do not always know exactly how to use them. I understand them well enough for reading, as a rule, but not for writing.

I am convinced that you will never know how much I love you and I sometimes regret that we cannot "turnabout" like Thorne Smith characters and experience each other's feelings, pleasures and love in order to be able to understand and appreciate our attachment for each other. Such an experiment would cast aside any doubts in your mind as to how I feel about remaining only yours for the rest of our lives.

Write me soon and remember that I think of you constantly (and pleasantly). I love you.

November 25, 1942

I haven't had a letter from you for around 10 days. I got a letter in yesterday's mail from one of Hazel's girls for an "unknown soldier" and I turned it over to Kessler for disposal. Told him to give it to some guy who'd write a nice letter back. If I don't get some mail pretty soon, I think I'll answer the next one myself under an assumed name. This place is so lonesome that nothing is too trivial to become a subject for conversation. The trees even whisper to each other every time a light breeze comes up.

Rupert the Great has a jeep now and is really king of the "campus". Both of us can't be gone at the same time and I am really in his good graces because I never go anywhere. That allows him to leave any time he pleases (which is often). There's no place I want to go.

We had a short meeting of officers the other night (the colonel got on us again for collecting into groups and shooting the bull at the dances, because he considers it ungracious to our guests) and after the meeting we went to a band concert that the artillery band played for our men. It was really a riot and I've not laughed so hard since I left home. You see, everyone is in the dark except the band who have Coleman lanterns to see by, and the boys take advantage of the comparative safety of darkness to unload some of their wit and humor which is always directed at the colonel.

I have to go now so will close. I'll finish this tomorrow. In the meantime, remember always that I love you.

November 26, 1942 – Thanksgiving Night
I am determined to celebrate the holiday in some way and writing to you is the only way I have as higher authorities arranged a very busy day that successfully precluded any opportunity for rest or recreation. I am often convinced that we have morale among the troops despite the shortsighted policies of some of our leaders rather than because of anything they do to promote it. If we were in combat or were doing anything that contributed even remotely to the success of any troops in combat, it would be entirely different. But we have spent the day in a normal manner just as though we were at Fort Clark and the colonel did not even call off retreat scheduled for the troops to be held in their own areas. And now we have to hurry to bed because we have to turn out at 4 a.m. for an overnight march.

It isn't that I mind for myself. I just feel that a half-holiday would have lent a little significance to the day in the minds of the men. If we have nothing to give thanks for (and I think we do have), then these boys are wasting their time, at the least, and their lives, at the most, for nothing. (I can't really say what I want to but you get the idea.) Better get some sleep before the march starts. I love you.

November 29, 1942
Since I wrote my letter #6 Thursday night I have really scored on mail and I will enumerate what I have received for your information (on the assumption that whatever makes me happy will also make you happy). First in importance was the receipt of three letters from you including one dated July 28 (unnumbered) and your #37 and #42 dated 11/1 and 11/17 respectively.

The letter from Dad made me feel good as his letters have an inexplicable way of doing. I suppose it's because he is so utterly naïve and straightforward that you unconsciously take his sincerity and love without any mental reservation.

We had another dance last night and it didn't turn out too well although I personally enjoyed it more than I have any of the others as I met several agreeable people and managed to talk at length for most of the evening. I danced some, too, and I find that you have the best conversations, and usually the best dancing, by sort of picking on the wallflowers.

The committee was a little upset as the Marine officers have monopolized the girls and gave all the nurses a cocktail party yesterday afternoon that kept most of them from getting to the dance at all. The Navy men have no camps where they can entertain effectively and, as a result, there are at least 50 or 75 at each of our parties. Since most of them are uninvited you can understand that most of those who come are a little on the boorish side and somewhat undisciplined. As they carry their liquor around on their ships with them, they are also more under the influence than most of the Army men.

This situation could easily lead to friction and probably will if the colonel doesn't work out some plan to keep them away. The whole thing seems sort of silly to me with a war going on but lots of them seem to have the "tomorrow we may die" attitude. I guess

Lloyd and some of his men in the primitive but comfortable environment of New Caledonia. New Guinea was to be altogether less bearable.

I'm the eternal optimist but I also feel that on some tomorrow I'll be coming home and I can't get worked up over a last fling.

I have felt unusually good all day today and got up early to work on my "front porch" that I started Thursday afternoon. I finished digging out the hillside and pitched the new fly and my tent is much nicer now. Especially it is cooler since the added shade is toward the prevailing direction of the wind and has a pre-cooling effect on it. We (Kessler and I) worked like dogs all morning and then I bathed and lay around all afternoon reading *Omnibook*.

During one particularly hot "session" last night someone of considerable experience suggested that this regiment would probably be moved to the Philippines after the war to replace the 26th Philippine Scouts which were virtually wiped out in the initial phases of the war. If that or any similar action is taken at the close of the war and I have the chance to stay in, I plan to do it and you could come over to be with me. I'm sure you feel the same way but I'd like to hear your views. We've seen both sides of the Army-Civilian question thoroughly, although I don't really feel the Army has had a fair showing due to abnormal circumstances.

It's getting late, so I will have to start closing. But I was anxious to answer your letter as your mail is so vital to me. Your letters make me awfully happy always and I'm trying to keep my "bread cast upon the waters". I love you.

December 1, 1942

I really didn't intend to write tonight, as I am tireder than I've been since we left Fort Clark. In fact, I finished supper and came over and hit the bunk for about 30 minutes debating the question before finally letting the flesh conquer the spirit. So, after deciding I just couldn't get across the tent under any circumstances, here I am writing a letter.

We got our second bubonic shot Sunday morning and Rupert had to go to bed yesterday afternoon and missed drill today too. It hasn't bothered me at all. Guess I'm pretty lucky although it hasn't seemed to bother anyone other than Rupert.

Kessler goes and gets my laundry, cigarets, etc. when I'm not around. He's a fine boy and it's almost like having Jary Jack with me to have him around. We put the finishing touches on my porte cochere this afternoon and I now have what is conceded to be the flossiest tent in the area. You'd be surprised at the pleasure I get from it.

I have put in a flowerbed around the fly and dug steps up the side of the hill. I went to the woods and dug up some spiny plants of the yucca type and transplanted them to the bed. They look swell so far and I hope to keep them alive. They look quite hardy and I think the chances are very good. I may get so good at gardening that I can take it over when I come home. Which can't be too soon for me. I love you.

The day that I dream of all the time is the day that I next get a glimpse of you and I am dedicating all my time to seeing that there will be not one minute cloud on the horizon of my homecoming. I want you physically from time to time, but when I compare that desire with my desire to be in the shelter of your loving presence it pales into a matter of comparatively little concern.

I guess we couldn't love each other as we do without there being a certain amount of jealousy involved. And, of course, you couldn't be so desirable to me without my thinking you could be equally desirable to someone else. And occasionally (not often, really) I let myself get a little afraid that you might grow tired of waiting for my mediocre charms and "give in" to some city slicker.

I'm just writing like this because I love you and miss you so much.

December 6, 1942

If I were an accomplished essayist you would be a very fortunate person as I certainly am a faithful correspondent whatever other virtues I may lack. Kessler was just in and saw me writing. Said to tell you "Merry Christmas". He never asks about you outright but usually brings my mail over and manages to find a job of some kind around my tent while I read it. I always try to read all the news aloud to him as he gets pretty lonesome at times.

Everything is fairly peaceful at "Camp Texas". The colonel has additional duties at the moment and just can't get around to gnaw on our fannies as he used to do. So, occasionally at least, there is a little rest for the weary.

Tomorrow will be the first anniversary of Pearl Harbor and it will be a year Tuesday since I moved out to the Mexican Border with Troop C. I recall that we were somewhat inconvenienced by the move coming as near to Christmas as it did.

But we knew then that it could become considerably worse, as it has. I find that I have the same philosophy now. Although the circumstances are, at best, "inconvenient", I never forget for a moment that they could still be worse than they now are.

I received the box yesterday with the camera, films, maple-leaf insignia, mantles, etc. and was really pleased. Everything I've been needing was in it. It certainly bucks me up to know that you are there waiting until you hear that I need something and then you get it for me and send it on over.

The camera is very fine and makes a picture of excellent size (2½ x 4½) which is larger by a considerable amount than the average "candid" type camera takes. This is far more practical here where the facilities for making enlargements just don't exist. I'm awfully pleased with it.

Liquor is out of the question over here now. Whiskey is going at $15 per quart when you can get it and some gin is available at $8 per quart. The brandy that I mentioned before has played out and can't be gotten at any price. So drinking is at a halt as far as most of us are concerned. That suits me fine. I had little taste for liquor when I got here and it grows lesser and lesser as I go withouter and withouter.

Knowing you as I do and feeling your love for me as I cannot help but feel it, I am certain that there is nothing you would rather have for a Christmas present from me than a pledge that I am all for you and will always be yours and yours alone. I love you.

December 7, 1942

My mail from the folks has fallen off considerably but I again assume that it is due to delay in transit, as Mama is a pretty fair correspondent as a rule. I find, by reading between the lines mostly, that they seem to think more of you every day. They make me feel a lot easier because they seem to feel that you are taking our separation and your pregnancy so bravely. Looks like it's all making a "man" of you, baby, and I appreciate it because it would worry me a lot to feel that you were going to pieces. We always seemed to be able to rise to the occasions though, didn't we?

This letter is getting hard to write as several sailors have joined me on my bench and are talking to each other as well as asking me questions about the island. The first question is always about where to buy whiskey. And that's easily answered, as there just flat isn't any to be had.

We had a very good lunch today – lovely fried fish with lime juice for the first course, then chowder, peas fried in bacon with lettuce, a small slice of beef roast and a fair sized piece of baked ham. Not bad either with plenty of French bread and tinned butter. No drink except water and a demitasse after we were through. We've been eating at the mess but the last meal we had there was so bad it scared us off.

I'm giving up for the moment as I see Stanley coming back. Write me soon. I love you.

December 11, 1942

I came back from supper tonight and found a bottle of Coke sitting on my footlocker in simple majesty. Of course, I have no ice but can enjoy the anticipation of it for a week or two until I can dig up some ice. Salome could do the dance of seven veils for me and it still wouldn't distract my watchful eye from that lovely example of Neo-American glassware.

I thought I was going to have a siege of dysentery but Captain Tascarella gave me 20 bismuth capsules and a tablespoonful of paregoric last night that put me back on my feet again. I have not missed a day of duty yet over here and don't intend to, as there is little excuse for sickness that I can see. Of course, an injury could put you out but they are no more liable here than at Clark now that the horses are becoming subdued.

I got a box from the folks yesterday containing tamales, pecan halves, candy, shrimp, etc. and was pleased, naturally. The tamales were especially welcome as the food has been particularly obnoxious the past few days.

I sent Christmas cards and seasonal V-mails to Platt and others here and there. It's funny how much you really mean your wishes at times like this. I'll be awfully disappointed if everyone doesn't have a swell Christmas. It's one of the things we're over here to insure, I guess, and we like to know we're accomplishing a little.

As for your Christmas presents, I selected each and every one of them personally from the catalog including color, weight, and size. It was a lot of fun and I hope you get half the pleasure from them that I got out of selecting them for you. It helped me pass many an hour that would have been pretty empty otherwise.

I've always enjoyed giving you things, you know, and I hope I always will. In fact, I enjoy it more than I do receiving gifts, as it has always been a little embarrassing to me for anyone to give me a present. I never have known why, either, as its naturally pleasant to be remembered. I've always felt pretty humble inside and I continue to be a little amazed when anyone goes out of the way to do me a kindness. The greatest kindness of all is your love. Write me soon. I love you.

December 17, 1942

I wrote to you Tuesday and wrote to the family via Dad Tuesday night and just before I finished my letter to him I found out I was going to make a reconnaissance trip of certain island outposts that are maintained by our troops. Lt. Hill is making the trip to carry rations, mail, pay, and supplies to the boys and I am going along for the ride. Or, to make it real military, I am going as an observer in order to familiarize myself with the country concerned.

We made a flying start (flying from one place to another doing the things we had overlooked the night before) Wednesday morning about 7:00 a.m. and had completed our visits to the first two of the outposts, about 40 and 60 miles away respectively, by 3:30 p.m. We had lunch at the first one we visited where they served us a delicious venison roast from a young deer they had killed the day before.

These outposts are all located where observation toward the sea can be maintained and are, of necessity, situated on high hills. These hills are so high and so steep that it took us 15 minutes of hard climbing (and resting) to reach the actual observation point and that was after we had driven the vehicles at least two-thirds of the way up to their base camp.

At 3:30 we filled our gas tanks (we have a jeep, two pickup trucks and two trailers) and started across the island on a narrow trail that threaded in and out through the mountains, hanging from their sides like a long and somewhat insecure balcony. Quite a thrill, too, as it was raining a great deal of the time and the roadway was slick in many places. Often we were above the clouds and looking down on them although the road took enough occasional dips into them and below them to wet us intermittently, then climbed back again to the chilling air above.

This is the most rugged bit of land I have ever seen. The whole island is mountainous. The few level areas are narrow, forming little more than a channel for the many creeks and rivers draining the hillsides. All the agriculture, which isn't a great deal, is done on the hillsides and the hills themselves seldom have a gentle slope. In fact, most of them are what I would consider as actually precipitous.

To get back to the trip, we arrived on the other side of the island at the village where we were to spend the night about

5:45 p.m. and took rooms at the hotel, where they served us a pretty good dinner. We got up this morning and went about ten miles up the coast to another outpost and spent the balance of the morning inspecting, unloading supplies, taking pictures and in making arrangements for a boat to take us down the coast the following day for more outpost inspections.

I enjoyed this visit more than any of the others as Ed Berry is in charge here and I was very glad to see him. He has shown quite a little ingenuity, especially for a corporal, in getting his camp set up and it looked to me like an ideal place to spend the rest of your life. He has hired two natives at 25¢ each per day (high wages, incidentally) to keep the place policed up and do the kitchen chores. They have built him a small native-type mess hall and erected an arbor with a thatched roof as a kitchen fly. The mess hall is screened with condemned mosquito bars and was very cozy, I thought. The natives have brooms they have made from tree limbs bunched together and tied and when Ed hollers "Police up!!!" they really start sweeping.

They also have a little pig named Julian that they purchased from a nearby Frenchman and are fattening up for Christmas. They prepare it a cooked breakfast of GI farina and feed it coconuts for the balance of the day. The use of the farina for pig feeding is another tribute to Ed's ingenuity as it is the first time in my nearly 13 years of military service that I have ever seen the stuff used to any practical end. Certainly the pigs are the first living things I have ever seen enjoy it.

Their two natives are cosmopolites by comparison to the others I have seen as they wear undershirts with their shorts and know enough about the Army to recognize various ranks. Both were in France during the First World War and returned to this place via New York.

After completion of the arrangements for tomorrow's trip, we unloaded a trailerful of supplies into the boat and returned to the hotel where we are now waiting for our supper. There is really no reason for us to stay at the hotel as all of us have adequate field equipment with us for camping. But the beds here are so comfortable and the food so different from the canned rations to which we have not become accustomed these past few months that we are staying here through tomorrow night, our plan being to lay over and rest from the boat trip.

As we emerged from the mountains yesterday afternoon and began our long and gradual descent toward sea level on this side of the island, the vegetation gradually grew more and more tropical in its nature. Here at the shores we are surrounded by an almost solid forest of palm and banana trees.

We have been gorging all day on coconuts and fresh bananas as well as pineapples, all of which we picked ourselves. Pineapples are the only fruit of the three that is cultivated by the natives as it grows from bushes. The others grow on trees and the natives just take them as they come. I was able to buy a medium-sized basket (woven from a palm frond) of pineapples from an old native couple for 10 francs (about 25¢) and gave them all the change that I had loose in my pockets, about 60¢, because I hated so badly to take advantage of them. There were twenty or more pieces of fruit in the sack and each of them was the equivalent of a 20 or 30 cent can of fruit there in the US.

The fruit here is much better than that we have become accustomed to eat at home as it is sun-ripened on the vine and the pineapples are especially good, having the same tart taste that we are accustomed to find only in strawberries. I've eaten five today, plus two bananas and a coconut. In addition, our dessert for dinner tonight consisted of an ambrosial dish made of chopped papaya pulp, shredded fresh coconut, pineapple and bananas, all covered over with passionfruit seeds. These are like large tomato seeds except that they have a rich flavor that I can only describe by saying that it tastes the way a sweetish sort of perfume smells. I have always heretofore associated exoticism with dark haired, slant-eyed girls but from now on the word will bring to mind the dessert I had tonight!

Hill and the four enlisted men that we brought along are all very pleasant companions. We have a sergeant who speaks some French, two drivers, and a private from the payroll section of regimental headquarters who is paying off the troops as we find them. All very jolly and lots of fun, but I miss you.

December 19, 1942

I arrived to find Kessler looking awfully lonesome. I know it must get pretty tiresome to him taking care of my stuff, but he still hangs around me all the time. He stayed here for over an hour while we opened the mail as I always hand him about half the letters I get to read. Of course, I only read parts of yours to him but most of the ones I get from home or from other places are just bits of news and gossip and he really drinks it all in. In fact, he gets more kick out of the cards than I do.

I brought him about 50 coconuts and 4 or 5 ripe pineapples when I came in and he's having a good time showing them around. I'm sorry I didn't get you to send him a little something for Xmas as he doesn't get a great deal of mail from anyone. And I really believe he's crazy about us both. And I certainly think a lot of him!

Off to the corral. I love you.

December 24, 1942

Well, here it is Christmas Eve – and by the time you get this you will probably be wondering why none of you have heard from me for the last several days. Well, the truth is that I have been in bed with a minor throat infection and, although I haven't been seriously ill, I've felt pretty bad and have lacked the energy to write to you. I've been having a little fever (only 2.5 degrees) for three days but I awakened this morning in a sweat and found my temperature to be normal. The doctor says I will be back to duty by Saturday morning, so don't worry about me any.

It is terribly hot today, as usual, although the nights are pretty cool and always require one blanket and, occasionally, two for comfort. Kessler has rolled the sides of my tent up and I'm getting all the breeze available.

I got two boxes yesterday: a box of candy from you mailed at Monnigs and a box from Striplings from Mama. I opened my boxes last night, as we are not going to celebrate the 25th. Kessler did the actual work and I listed the contents of each on the back of the card it contained. I won't try to list them now as I still feel a little too poorly for bookkeeping.

There's been an intermission since I wrote the foregoing during which I have eaten two pretty good-sized meals: dinner and supper, both turkey with trimmings. I feel a lot better now with something under my belt and it didn't hurt me at all to eat even though I'd stuck to fruit juice for two days. Incidentally, the fruit juice that you all included in my packages came in handy as that is what I've had to sustain me. Orange juice, apple, pineapple and tomato – a very nice assortment and especially welcome because we don't get any juice except grapefruit, which, as you know, I don't like.

I've not been able to work up a great deal of Christmas spirit. However, it has been a very happy day. Christmas is necessary in ordinary times, I suppose, to remind people that they should be thoughtful of those they love – and that someone somewhere loves them. But it isn't necessary over here for the simple reason that you fall back on your love for others and their regard for you every day in order to better stand the successive unpleasantnesses. You come to depend upon this so much that there is no great reserve of love or understanding left for a special day like Christmas. It's sort of like this talk about taking silver out of the Treasury and putting it to every day tasks to help win the war. We've just taken our reserve of love and kindness and thoughtfulness for others out of the treasury where we ordinarily keep it very carefully (and, often, unused) and put it to the useful task of maintaining our morale so we can keep going no matter what comes to discourage us.

There was a regimental formation this morning with the band, and sacks of candy, chewing gum, cigarets and cigars were handed out to everyone. The boys all appreciated the fact that it had been packed, because it indicated that someone had been thoughtful of them and had done all they could to give them a good Christmas. As I've often told you, the thought behind gifts is much more valuable to us than their intrinsic value. The most important feeling when you get a package is one of pleasure that someone has thought of you; the next in importance (usually) is gratitude that whoever sent it had enough sense to send something useful instead of just something expensive.

This second thought springs from two sources, the first being because we need things every day that we don't have and also because it indicates that some time and thought has been put into the selections. I've been told that in some parts of China soap is valued in the hundreds of dollars per cake and, although we have plenty of soap here, we have shortages of things that can easily help me to imagine that it is true. Fortunately, we are short of nothing absolutely essential to maintaining ourselves in a reasonable condition.

Write me soon, Virginia, and let me know how you're doing, as I am really anxious about you and think of you almost every minute. After all, I'm pretty much unaccustomed to being an expectant father. I just hope I love the baby half as much as I love you.

December 26, 1942

As a very special Christmas present, I received your letters numbered 45 and 51 of 11/22 and 12/12. Nothing could have been nicer as I must confess that Christmas was an anticlimax. And that is an insult to the day because no one had expected much, anyhow. We did have lots of good turkey but with results I will describe. I also received a *Life*, a *Newsweek* and two *Saturday Evening Posts* and then got another *Newsweek* today.

One of the nicest features of the day was the Taps last night which was played by an ensemble from the band twice, once loud and sweet and then again, softly as if in the distance.

As I told you, we had our turkey on Christmas Eve and that night 25 or more members of Troop A almost simultaneously turned up deathly sick. It was during the picture show and, as I had not gone to the show, I was the first officer notified. I soon found that you could not hold 25 heads at once and got the doctor over with his detachment, so left them to it, returning only occasionally to see what progress they were making. At about 12:50, when we thought Troop A to be well in hand, Troop B turned up en masse with diarrhoea. Some fun!! We dispensed bismuth pills and paregoric to them until about 2:00 at which time I took a sedative and went to bed. The last thing that I recall hearing was 5 or 6 B troopers en route to the latrine singing "Praise the Lord, and pass the toilet paper".

No doubt we'll feel like a million dollars tomorrow. I love you.

Daddy's approved form of communication to Virginia, a long chatty letter, banged out on his old high-backed Remington.

Saturday evening,
25 December 1941.

Dearest Virginia:

I don't seem to like to use a typewriter any more. I really don't
know why. But, since I have this new one out anyhow, I've just knocked off a
short note to you. I bet she machine out because I wanted to write to
your grandmother and felt that she could probably read typing more easily than she could my indecipherable hand.

As a very special Christmas present, I received your letters numbered 44 and 45 or 11/32 and 12/13. Nothing could have been nicer as I
had hoped that Christmas was an exciting time. And that is an insult to
that abstract day because no one had reported much, anyhow. We did have lots of
good turkey but with results that I will describe later. I also received
a life, a Cavalcade and a few more that were last night which has played an impossible picture for the band later, once I had read every now and then again
madly as if in the distance.

As I believe I told you, we had our turkey Christmas dinner in
the night that night. 25 or more members of Troop A almost simultaneously
turned up deathly sick. It was during the picture edition I soon found that
was gone to the show, I was the first officer. And I was found that
we could not hold my hands at once and get the doctor over with its de-
tachments and left it to them returning only occasionally to see what progress that they were making. At about 12:30, when we thought Troop A is
is well in hand, Troop B turned up an even with Sickness. The last thing that I remember that I sup-
which when I took a sedative and went to bed. The last thing that I re-
posed dispensed himself pills and paregoric in them until about 2:00
we dispensed himself pills and paregoric to them until about 2:00
can't hearing the 3 or 4 troopers on route to the latrine singing "Praise
the Lord, and pass the toilet paper."

Everyone was OK next day although I had a slight fever return and
had to spend one hour day in bed. Did a days duty today through without
very difficulty and feel like a million dollars at the moment.

I was pleased to hear that the girls had been over there you.
Can tell you that you'll need a map so know what we are going to do
the rest of the war. We are going to sit over here and stagnate, while
for troops goddarned forces for the rest of the war. And darnfool anybody kid say that they are disappointed though they are all

1943

January 2, 1943

Here I am, home from the hospital and as well as I've ever been in my life. I thought I was OK last weekend but rode in a review Monday and my horse was so rambunctious that it upset me and gave me a fever. My throat was almost well at the time so my stay in the hospital was something in the nature of a rest cure. It was especially helpful since I was completely away from any responsibilities here and could just relax and read all day and sleep at night.

New Year's Eve was a little dismal as there were only about four of us in there, the rest having slipped off somewhere. The other three were one lieutenant who was married and didn't want to slip out and a couple of officers with a tropical fungus disease who couldn't slip out. We stayed up and kept the lights on until 10, and that was a sort of hell-raising gesture as they are supposed to be out by 9 sharp. There were a couple of new doctors fresh from S.F. staying in the officers' ward temporarily while their baggage was being brought out from town. We enjoyed hearing about the steaks they had before leaving S.F.

and the nightclubs they attended and they got a kick out of the stories the boys were able to tell about their flying experiences in the Solomons.

To avoid any misunderstanding about this baby naming business, I'm not particularly fond of the name Anne but just used it to suggest possible combinations like Carol Anne, Virginia Anne, etc. Sue is the same type of name and I like it just as well. You know: Mary Sue, etc. I just offered them as illustrations of a type of name and not because I preferred any of them to any other. This baby is going to be practically all yours anyhow so you can just name it to suit yourself! I'm serious though when I say that I've never been overly fond of Sam or Lloyd either. If it's a boy, I like Gary fine and have no objection to it, nor to its being named after Mrs. Cunningham. (You might name it "Gary Baldy" and include him, too.) Incidentally, my maternal grandmother was named Laura. I like Laura Sue as well as Laura Anne. Either goes nicely with Hunnicutt.

I agree with the doctor that you should stay out of crowds. Something might happen to hurt you and that would mess things up generally. I don't want you scared by an automobile or anything this late – the baby might have a voice like a Chevrolet horn!

Well, baby, it won't be very long now until you'll be relieved of your burden and I'll be happy and relieved when it is all over with. I've worried some although you've done a pretty fair job of convincing me that you are not doing badly.

I do love you so very much, and want so much to be with you that it's a little hard to take at times. But there'll be a day—!! I love you.

January 6, 1943

I've been pretty "antsy" lately about being away from you. Of course, it always bothers me but I usually keep it under better control. I miss you so much that I wish they'd hurry up and turn us loose on the Japs. It might speed things up a little!

I'm still gnawing on the peach covered toffee. I've eaten all the other candy that I got for Christmas but I have been mighty conservative on those and have saved most of them for my own personal use. You can't afford to pass candy like that around!

I don't think I mentioned *Life,* but I received one of those, too. One of the officers that I know over here had his wife burned to death in the Boston fire and pictures of it were in the copy I got. They had a young baby, so he was flown home immediately. Sure was tough. I'd go nuts if anything happened to you and I sure want you to be careful of yourself especially now when I imagine you must be a little awkward.

Well, I'm out of gas tonight and the candlelight is pretty dim. I'm a little tired and nervous, too, so will bring this to a close. Not a very good letter but I'm hurried because I have to get ready for the march in the morning.

Give my regards to your grandmother and both our families. I just can't seem to get much time for writing except to you. Want to thank everyone for my nice Christmas. Write soon. I love you.

January 7, 1943 – V-mail

I slept pretty lightly last night and dreamed a good deal about you. I seldom dream at all and can't remember just what I dreamed last night – but I awakened with a pleasant feeling of having been near you that helped a lot to ease my constant sense of loneliness.

I feel certain I'll have some mail from you as we get in from this trip and will be glad to hear how you're doing. I don't believe I was ever more interested – which I'm sure is only natural at this time. The anxieties of fatherhood are really getting me down.

Gotta go now. Be sweet and remember that I love you very much.

January 9, 1943

Rupert had to go to the hospital this morning as it appears he has some more ribs fractured. Haven't heard the results of his X-rays yet, though. He and Ed went into town for a swim yesterday afternoon and I understand that they had a few "quick ones" on the way at some point or other. I don't know just how he hurt himself exactly and Ed professes not to know either. Guess I'll have to take the old man's abuse for a few days.

We have two problems [manoeuvres] coming up for next week, one an all nighter. I just wonder if Rupe didn't see the drill schedule before he decided his ribs were broken. That's always the time for the heat to be turned on. I don't mind, as I can't see that I have anything to lose. The colonel has been pretty pleasant to me lately, anyhow – that is, pleasant for him.

I'm awfully anxious to hear about your Christmas. I realize that it is pretty hard for you to be happy under the circumstances but I tried awfully hard to make you as happy as possible. Of course, it was all selfish on my part because I've got lots of fun from the occasional things I've been able to give you these past few years. And, also, I want to keep you happy because happiness keeps you young – and I don't want to come home and find a wrinkled, dowdy old woman waiting for me!

That's selfishness, too, but not altogether, as I want our baby to be raised in a happy home with parents that it won't be ashamed of as old fogies. If I stay in the Army, it will be primarily for the financial security involved. We're getting (I am, anyhow) spoiled on the money question and I certainly don't want to go back to our early-married status where we had to scrape and save all the time.

I want the balance of our lives to be free from financial worry. Especially since I don't think we'll ever have any other kind of trouble. If we don't love and appreciate each other enough by now to live happily together after this mess is over, then we don't deserve any future happiness.

I know that I could play around over here from time to time. But my love for you is strong enough to keep me from being tempted. I just don't have the desire to go out with other women at all so I don't even get any credit for overcoming temptation.

Not very heroic but it's a very satisfactory condition so far as I am concerned. I think that having the desire to be untrue is just one jump short of the actual deed. Every man has to decide these things for himself and each undoubtedly sets up his own criterion by which he governs himself. My own set of rules has been simple. I first say, "Would Virginia object?" and "Would I object if Virginia did the same thing?" I guarantee that one or other of those questions will stop anything that is remotely questionable – if you listen to the true answer that your heart gives you. You know what my heart always says. I love you.

January 12, 1943

The latest news is that the government is going to pay a $250.00 uniform allowance to all who were inducted below the grade of major which will be a little hard to take. I want ours kept separate from all other funds to pay for a trip for us "after the war". You might as well reconcile yourself to their including enlisted service in accounting for longevity which means that I add 2 fogies or 10% monthly to our already tax burdened income. That will make 4 fogies altogether instead of the 2 we get at present – a total of 20% per month ($50.00) as longevity making my base $300, plus $25 overseas, plus $105 rent, plus $63.00 rations – less $300 to you, $37.50 bonds, $7.30 insurance and $18.60 rations.

Of course it may be some time before this all trickles through but it shouldn't take over a couple of months at the most. It should be enough extra altogether to almost pay for the baby, don't you think, with a lump sum of $250.00 plus the $25.00 per month. Incidentally, when I send money home, be sure to tell me when you receive it including the amount of the m.o. as well as the number of it so I can destroy my receipt and quit worrying.

I'm sorry I can't send more but I feel sure you've received the allotments by now although I still haven't heard since I was in the hospital. I wrote the bank to let you have what you need and feel sure that they will do so if you ask them for it. I don't know whether you got the apartment or not but hope you have it all set for yourself when you get out of the hospital.

I want terribly to be with you these next few weeks although I realize that I would be of little, if any, help and my only comfort is that I know you will be well taken care of in every way. I'm sure you are happy that the long months of waiting are coming to a close and that you will soon have a baby to love and care for. Of course, I am happy about it, too, and I know that I'm going to be all agog until I hear that everything has "come out" satisfactorily. When it gets a little rough I hope it will help for you to remember that I love you.

January 16, 1943 (afternoon)

I got two letters from Mama last night that brought me as much pleasure as any I've received since I left home because the first told me all about their preparations for Christmas and the second, about your receiving your gifts.

Of course, I haven't heard from you since before Christmas but, in a way, I'm glad as Mama told me how happy you seemed to be over your gifts and how surprised you were. She seemed to think that you got a real thrill out of everything and that naturally pleased me, as I had wanted you to enjoy the things so much. Also she told me that she had never seen you prettier than you were that day and that your complexion was gorgeous (apparently that is a sign that you are getting along well).

Mama has worked so hard at being a mother to us in every way that it especially pleased me to receive a letter telling me what a good, sensible and loving mother you were going to be. You would have almost thought that I had intimated something to the contrary and Kessler and I both laughed when I read it out loud to him. I certainly wouldn't dare even hint that you were lacking in any of the virtues, else I'd have my family and yours both on my neck!!

I'm pleased that the apartment deal seems to be going nicely. I'll be much happier knowing that your mother will be "on call" just across the street if you need her for anything. I don't think anything much is apt to turn up that you can't handle for yourself but it's nice to have them so close. Especially since I know she is so willing to help.

I get awfully worried about you and the baby at times and it's nice to realize that everything is as good as it is. It could be so very much worse and I feel truly thankful and fortunate that we are as well situated as we are. With all my worrying, though, the whole thing is a little unreal at times. It is difficult to remember you as having been pregnant when I left and the whole thing is somewhat like I feel when I'm reading a particularly vivid and gripping novel. I can't explain it better than that but I'm sure you understand what I mean.

I know that I'll be on needles and pins for the next three weeks until I hear that you and the baby are safe, but I'm really happy that it will be here soon and that you'll finally have what you have wanted so badly these past few years. Nothing makes me happier than for you to have something that you want and I guess that can only be because I love you.

January 17, 1943

I won't overburden you with my thoughts tonight as they are going to show *Holiday Inn* and, if the reviews I've read can be trusted, it's one of the best shows of the year. You've probably seen it – has Bing Crosby, Mary Martin and, I think, Bob Hope.

There is a song over here the gist of which is expressed by a line saying, "There'll be no promotion this side of the ocean." Of course, there can be but little promotion except where new units are being organized and I suppose it is somewhat unfair to us, although I personally have no complaint.

Anyhow, we hear that any officer who completes his six months in grade in foreign service and who is recommended by his CO for promotion but for whom there is no vacancy in the next higher grade here, will be sent home, promoted one grade and reassigned to a unit that is alerted for movement to a similar area to the one he has previously been assigned. This will give deserving officers a promotion and will give units to which they are assigned an officer experienced in the items required where they are going; how their materiel should be packed; how to load ship, embark, etc. Anyhow, it makes a good rumor and rumors are all we have to keep us stimulated. So we enjoy them whether we believe them or not!

I know that one of the letters I write in the next few days is the letter that you'll be reading in the hospital before long. I don't know how to write one that is "appropriate" but I will try to write enough to keep you from being too lonesome for me. But, whether I have the time to write all I'd like and whether the letters are appropriate to the occasion or not you can be sure all the time that I'll be thinking of you and of the baby and will be loving you both with all my heart and soul and body. And I'll be wishing I could be there with you to bring you things, and rub your back, and make your breakfast toast and coffee as I have sometimes done before. I love you.

January 18, 1943

We are starting on an even harder schedule than before now. Putting a 5-day week into effect – that is, we work 5 days with no time off (7 to 5) and then rest the sixth day. Of course, the men can't rest all day the sixth day, as they have to put out their washing that day. Altogether a little rough for cavalry, I'd say. Of course, my attitude, as usual, is that if they don't have any better sense than to order it then I don't have any better sense than to try to see that it is carried out.

The new 5-day week is working – working the hell out of us! Makes it a little rough in spots but nothing we can't stand. We'd all appreciate it more if we thought it was doing any damage to the Japs! Since it isn't, it sometimes seems a little futile.

I took a very cold shower after the show and am pretty thoroughly relaxed or would be if the mosquitoes would leave me alone. They are at their worst at this season. I counted 23 on Bill

Laird at one time today. Fortunately, their bites just itch a little but they don't carry malaria and they don't raise whelps on you. They sure knock the romance out of correspondence, though, as it is pretty hard to sit still and concentrate with a dozen or more of them biting on you. And I'm not even mildly exaggerating.

My letters ramble on from day to day and I want you to know that it hasn't gone this way because there has been any lull in my ever-present and ever-growing love for you. I just have to quit before the mosquitoes make me so nervous that I can't go to sleep. When you undress and get under the bar there are enough of them on you that you can't get rid of them all and a few always get cooped up with you.

I go to court again today for the second trip this week and know of one more session due, at least; it is still a change for me. I should smell pretty good this trip as I uncorked a bar of the fancy soap you sent me for my bath last night and my shave this morning. Quite luxurious, I think, having such fancy soap so far from civilization. And, of course, I still have my Old Spice, too.

Be sure to write as often as you feel like it, because I'm a little worried. I love you.

January 21, 1943

I'm sitting on the same park bench from which I wrote you once before after court. We got through by noon, had a very good lunch – steak, fried potatoes, cucumbers, some kind of macaroni mess, ice cream and coffee. Quite a feast for us, especially the ice cream, to which we are totally unaccustomed. It's made of goat's milk but was cold and well flavored.

The change in size and mode of writing is not to be construed by any manner of means a change in my editorial policy. This is just the kind of paper that was on sale today. Subscribers to my "Lonely Hearts" club may continue to expect the same old baloney.

We are having a very cool day and there are no mosquitoes, so that I am suffering only the distractions incident to sitting in a crowded public park with a few hundred other people as I try to concentrate. I figured that a short letter would let you know I was thinking of you, though, and this is it.

There is a taxi stand nearby whose customers are almost all sailors in various degrees of drunkenness. Some are quite amusing although most are not.

Nothing of consequence continues to happen 24 hours a day over here and most of the boys would welcome a little excitement. I don't think anyone would be particularly worried if we were ordered to an actual combat zone. I'm inclined to feel about this trip like the soldier who, as his ship passed under the Golden Gate Bridge, said, "This is carrying a rumor too far."

I'd like to come home and I miss you so terribly that I fight to keep from realizing it. However, I'd almost rather stay here for the rest of the war than to be sent home to a new unit and have to leave again after a short time. I'd know next time from experience exactly how hard it was going to be to stay away. Of course, if I got to come home for a while, we could start a little brother on the way for the baby!

Here comes our car so I'll have to quit for a while. Write me as often as you can. Mail has been awfully scarce since before Christmas, it seems, and I miss it very much. I love you.

January 23, 1943

This was the first "rest day" of our new schedule and everyone took the fullest possible advantage of it after five hard days that included eight hours of training daily in addition to housekeeping and horsekeeping, laundry, etc.

I put in the day until 3 p.m. on a reconnaissance. Took Bill with me to look for a campsite for a five-day ride next week. We had to locate water for the horses and that is not always easy, especially near the shore where the streams of any consequence are salty and rise and fall with the tide. We found a New Zealand outfit located on a lovely "bay-let" just the right distance away and with a well that they claim will furnish all the water we can pump out of it. We got there just at lunch and they invited us in to eat. We had a fine time with them and then went with them to meet the man who owns the land we were to camp on.

The Frenchman who owns the land invited us in for a drink and was pleased that we were planning to spend a couple of days with him. He had a very attractive wife and a cute girl about 12 and a boy about 7 or 8. I know they are going to be nice to us and feel sure we'll have a good trip.

We had gathered some wild limes (just like "tame" ones) on the way up and the major in command of their battalion carried all of us to his tent (that is, Bill, me and his own officers) and added a little gin from his last bottle to the juice of our limes.

You should see me now trying to concentrate on this letter. I have my shoes and leggings on to keep the mosquitoes off my ankles and I have my head net tied around my lower face and neck with nothing sticking out except my eyes. A little suffocating, but much better than being slowly eaten by a bunch of carnivorous flying turkeys, you can bet.

Rupert came back today from the hospital with a note prescribing at least 14 days dismounted duty. He hasn't told the colonel yet and I'm sure it's not going to go over too well as you can probably guess from past experience.

I'm having a good time with the squadron. Rupe wants to come home so badly that it would be a good thing if he got to and then maybe I could have the squadron all the time. I feel sure the colonel is due to come home for promotion or else get one over here before many months pass.

When I say one person "wants to come home" more than another, I merely mean that their morale is lower than that of the rest of us. Naturally, all of us are anxious to return but realize that we have to kick ourselves in the pants and keep going as long as we are assigned to duty over here. We'd certainly play hell with the war if everyone decided to throw in the sponge!

There's no use in my trying to tell you how much I long to be there to help you through these last few weeks. I'm sure you know all I could say and then, too, it will probably all be over by the time you get this.

Albright found out about his baby this week (a 9 lb 10 oz girl) and Lt. Tucker heard about his (also a girl) today. Looks like ours will almost be an anti-climax, as will Phil's. (Boy, does he want to go home!)

Judging by the list of things you mentioned having purchased, we could have twins with just one more dozen diapers! I'm sure glad we are able to have all of the things you need and the best that are available. I only hope that we can always maintain such a standard for our child until it is able to have a home of its own.

Well, this is 6¢ worth and I close reluctantly, if not more so. Of course, I must add those priceless words, especially now. I love both of you!

January 26, 1943

We awakened yesterday to find 17 of our 19 horses had flown the coop, and you can imagine my embarrassment. We finally found them all although several, including my own, were 10 or 12 miles away. I guess they're just not completely "civilized" as yet.

The colonel relieved Rupert of the squadron this morning and turned it over to me "indefinitely". (That's the word he used.) This doesn't mean anything definite for me as the colonel probably relieved him on account of his present dismounted status. As the colonel put it (a little bluntly, I thought), "You can't run a cavalry from an arm chair."

Well, I'm back from the Court Martial business and have an old oat sack burning here in my tent. It keeps the pests out and I'm freer of them than I've been for days. Of course, I can't see because the smoke tends to blind me, but that is a small price to pay.

We had fresh meat today and I ate an enormous sirloin steak, well done, with potatoes, bread and gravy, and pickles, with canned apricot halves for dessert. I'm probably as contented at the moment as it is possible for me to be and still be away from you.

I believe you know me well enough to know that I don't really dislike field soldiering although I would like a few of the simpler comforts in life occasionally. I don't get lonesome for liquor or excitement or, especially, for female company. It does hurt like hell at times, though, to look ahead to the bare months without you. It isn't all selfishness, either, as I hate your wasting a year or so of your life just waiting there for me. The only consolation that I have is that I wouldn't consider having it any other way – and I feel as honor bound to save myself and my love for you as I feel you should do for me. I'd be furious if you accepted the attention of other men and I can't see any excuse for me to play around and still feel that way about you.

I'm not narrow minded enough to think that it actually makes any physical difference, of course, but I do think it tarnishes your outlook and detracts from the honesty and fineness of committed love. And our love is just too perfect to let a passing fancy splash mud on it. (I don't really know what brings this on except that there are not many ways to say "I love you" and I enjoy the occasional realization that I just flat don't give a damn about any woman anywhere besides you.)

Mama mailed me a letter the 8th that also came yesterday and she repeated about your fine appearance, clear complexion and bright eyes. It certainly made me feel good to read it. I know they'll be crazy about the baby and will do all they can to spoil it, especially since it will be their "one and only". Spoiling it with love and gifts and happy surroundings will suit me so long as it is reasonably disciplined and well mannered. I never could believe that it is necessary to live a life of hardship as a preparation for success. Persons who rise above their surroundings to a higher level seem to me to be the type who would have gone even further with a better start in life.

(There will now be a short interruption while I drag my dead outfit to afternoon drill.)

January 28, 1943

Sorry for my delay in finishing this letter. I'm afraid we're going to be reduced to V-mail in the near future and it will be a damned dirty shame as letters go a long way toward keeping the boys happy. Certainly, they have no other "luxury" that will even begin to replace a good, long letter from home. V-mail will greatly reduce the mailing of military secrets, I must admit, as there just isn't room for the salutations and a military secret on just one sheet of the stuff.

Rupe is really in hog heaven now with his temporary relief from the squadron. He sits around resting on his dead fanny all day and tells us how to do. He's much better at explanation than at demonstration, it would seem.

I can't help but be a little scared about you. It's not a bad thing, either, because it makes me realize again and again how crazy I am about you. And also reminds me that I married you primarily to live with you always and not to have babies. No baby could be worth anything happening to you – and I can say that even though I do want us to have babies badly. My first loyalty will always be to you no matter what other claims there are upon me to anyone else (including the War Department!).

I can tell it's about time to get out and start inspecting because it is beginning to shower again. It will really start to pour in a few minutes and then I'll know to get under way. It's much more reliable to follow the rain than the bugle because the bugler is a human being (or, at least, a reasonable facsimile thereof) and is subject to an occasional error.

Be careful of yourself, sweetheart, and remember every moment that I'm thinking of you because I love you.

February 2, 1943

I have personally seen every little horsey watered and put to bed and it's now after 8 p.m. so I am going to depend upon the generosity of the War Department in general and old "squash head" in particular and presume to use a few precious minutes of the day for my own personal pleasure. That pleasure, of course, is the pleasure I always get from writing to my baby (you, I mean!).

I'll have to admit that my letters to you have been somewhat of a task recently due in part to the distractions that I have as squadron CO as well as the ever-present mosquitoes. The real trouble is that I can't think of anything when I am writing to you except of your condition and of the approaching birth of our baby. (A soldier on leave, upon starting back to camp just one jump ahead of being AWOL gave his section on the Pullman to a young lady and was delayed beyond the expiration of his pass. He wired his captain as follows: "Gave berth to a girl. Will return tomorrow." The CO wired back and said, "Congratulations. Your next confinement will be in the guard house.")

I took the squadron to the field today and thought we had a pretty good day. I thought up a mission that would cause the troops to camp separately and I think the captains all enjoyed having their troops to themselves. In the process of touring the various campsites in my jeep, I acquired the most gorgeous bunch of bananas you ever saw. The bunch actually has about 4 to 5 dozen bananas on it which makes it commonplace as far as numbers go – but you should see the bananas!! Each one about 8 inches long and as big around as my flashlight. They are still green as gourds (which is the way all bananas are picked) and their skins are so waxy smooth as to make them look artificial. I have them hanging under my tent fly where I can watch them because I intend to eat every one of them myself. Thieves, beware!!

I also brought a few mangoes and found them very flavorful. They are shaped like a plum, as big as a baseball, yellow as an orange, have a skin that resembles an apple's in texture and taste like peaches preserved in perfume. Very tart and almost draw your mouth up like a persimmon. We don't get many chances to have fruit, but I always try to buy all I can get.

The first bunch of bananas I bought cost 10 francs (25¢); the stuff I bought today (1 stalk of bananas and 1 dozen mangoes) cost nearly $3. Just a little local profiteering by our colleagues, the Filthy French. However, I don't want you to get the wrong idea – I don't think any less of them than I do of the Japs or Germans.

We're having hell with our lanterns lately as we only get red gas which clogs them badly. Reading at night is almost out of the question and letter writing isn't too easy. But I've got plenty of candles stored away to help keep my "communiqués" coming so I don't pay much attention.

I've either got to stop writing by this light or else become cross-eyed. If I was sure the baby had been born, I wouldn't worry about becoming cross-eyed but I wouldn't want it to happen before it's born as it might inherit them. (You know, I'm a great believer in heredity and environment and believe they are essential. My old saying when I was studying sociology was "A bad environment is certainly better than no environment at all.")

We still get lots of rumors over here, but they are not as good as they used to be and most of them are easily disproved. For instance, many of the guys are going around claiming the mosquitoes bite them through their boots. Now, my boots look like they had just recovered from smallpox and not a mosquito has been able to bore all the way through them yet although the evidence is there to prove that they tried! I love you.

February 5, 1943

I'm really ashamed of my recent efforts as a correspondent but I seem to be able to do little if anything about it.

I've never felt more in love with you than I have these past few weeks nor have I ever been more inclined to think of you and wish to be with you. Under the circumstances, I feel that it is only normal for me to feel this way and I had hoped that as the time approached for the baby to be born, I could really try to make you realize my feelings.

Somehow, I've failed to do it, though, and I want to tell you why just for fear you might get the mistaken idea that I'm becoming accustomed to being away from you. I just can't get the peace and quiet that is necessary for me to try to write the things I want to tell you. There is no place to escape the mosquitoes except by going to bed under a mosquito bar where it is impossible to write.

I honestly believe that they constitute the most nerve-wracking experience I have ever known. I am only thankful that I have learned to be patient and to relax a little under pressure and am in good physical condition.

I wanted you to have a love letter from me every day you were in the hospital – each a reminder to you of how I love you and longed to be with you when you needed me the most.

The doctors all claim that a husband is the most useless thing there is at a child birth but I am sure I could do a lot for you if I were there. I could bring you flowers and be the referee between you and the nurses when you're being neglected.

It's a funny thing, but the nearer the baby gets to us, the less concerned I feel with it and the more anxious I feel about you and your welfare. The most important thing in the world to me is *you* – and our life together has been too lovely for any other person or thing, even our own child, to interfere with it or replace you in my heart.

I want you to have children and I know that I will love them and care for them to the fullest degree – but that love and care will be a love that I'll have for them separate and apart from my feelings for you because I know that I can't divide my love for you to include anything else. It's too strong for that.

Many people claim that children are necessary to insure a happy home but I don't remotely believe it in our case. I think that they will prove to be a tremendous joy and satisfaction to us but I'm just as sure that my love for you would have continued on into eternity, as I am sure I love you now. (And that's being pretty certain!)

Try to understand why I'm so distracted in my correspondence and remember that the work I'm doing, often under handicap, is equally for you and the baby. I never wanted success and promotion so much before and I intend to bend every effort to attain them.

If we were together I'd be willing to ease up on my military in order to have some sort of home life and if I never got a promotion, I'd call it square. But, since we are separated anyhow, I intend to push myself and my work to the limit of my ability.

I am sometimes almost crazy with loneliness and desire for you and usually a good long letter will sort of serve to cure me. But not tonight, it seems, so I'll just have to give up anyhow. I love you.

February 16, 1943

I suppose I should be very excited right now as I got a cable about the baby today at noon. I'm awfully proud to be a father, of course, but mostly right now I'm happy to feel that you've been relieved of your burden that I know has made the going pretty rough for you these past few months. But it makes me feel helpless to realize that anything can happen over there and I can't know about it – birth, death, accident – literally anything, and I am completely powerless. It's sure frustrating not to be there to try to take care of my family.

I suppose that after the war is over and I've been home a few years this little jaunt will become somewhat insignificant but it certainly isn't that way now.

The information that I got via the Red Cross is pretty meager and all I actually know is that we have a girl. Well, we requisitioned for a girl so I certainly can't complain on that score. I know you're very happy about it and I believe that it will help you a lot to pass the time quickly until I can get back home.

I'm sure that Mama has picked a good college for it by now. (In fact, if she hasn't started planning its life, it will be a sure sign she doesn't care anything about it.)

I received a box from the folks today with wooden beach sandals, a carborundum rock for sharpening my knife, and a bunch of flower seeds. All were welcome but the flower seeds were most timely as I can plant them around the mess hall.

The troopers refer to the hall as the "Epidemic Building" as the colonel named it the "Academic Building". They refer to our dances as "Rat Races". Kessler saw me going to bathe and wanted to know if I was going to the rat race. He seemed quite pleased when I told him I wasn't and carried my razor off, supposedly to polish it up – but I suspect it was so that I couldn't possibly change my mind.

I hope the lone (and somewhat forlorn) picture of me got by the censors OK. Getting that picture developed was somewhat like the mountain laboring to bring forth a mouse.

We got a replacement in Troop C named Huffaker from Knoxville, Tennessee, and I just had him down for a short visit. Huffaker was Mama's maiden name and, if I recall correctly, her family came from Tennessee. You might mention it to her as I am much too tired to write home tonight and we go out on a two-day problem tomorrow.

Well, my rags are burning out so I'd better get to bathing and get under my mosquito bar for a little (I hope) peace and quiet. This sounds like an exaggeration, but is the absolute truth – after you get the net tucked in, the mosquitoes buzz around and around it with a sort of a frustrated noise very similar to the noise of a vacuum cup tie on a heavily loaded truck speeding downhill. I'm telling you the truth when I say that I've never seen mosquitoes so thick, so large or so determined to bite you.

Be careful of yourself, sweetheart, and remember every moment that I'm thinking of you, because I love you.

February 19, 1943

Got in from our 2-day maneuver today and found the cable from your mother regarding the baby and was awfully glad to get. It reassured me considerably coming from the family as it did. Also it had the date which gave me something concrete as "evidence". I got some of the kick out of that I had expected from the first one.

This is an amazing Saturday for me as we have not only skipped calisthenics but are not even having an inspection. It's hard to believe, I know, and many feel that it's a definite indication that the colonel is failing mentally and physically. I still stick to my normal conviction that underneath it all, he is really human and is just giving us a break after a couple of hard days.

We had one of the best shows last night that I have seen in some time. It was *Take a Letter, Darling* with Rosalind Russell and Fred McMurray. La Russell was all glamoured up but McMurray really put the show over. It was a good tonic for a bunch of tired guys. I almost didn't go, which would have been bad, as I needed it.

We are able to get canned cigarets now that are much fresher than the packaged ones to which we have been accustomed. They are much nicer to our mouths and certainly are more enjoyable to the palate. Incidentally, the last cigarets you sent have never arrived but I feel sure that they will show up eventually.

I am enclosing the two messages I've had so far about the baby to be put in its baby book. I hear from home that Mama has one all fixed up for it which I think is swell. I sent Mama a little money to use for anything she thought suitable and she planned to send flowers. I hope she did and that you enjoyed them. I completely overlooked Valentine's Day to my complete and utter shame. I'll think of it often enough, though, as it is about time for me to start getting magazines with Valentine covers, ads, and articles. The ones I've been getting the past few weeks still have Christmas dope in them – makes it a little confusing!

I have to go to the critique now so will close this. I hope to hear more about you and the baby soon although I must confess that the baby seems somewhat unreal to me so far. The thoughts I've had of you and your pain and danger have certainly been real enough. Anyhow, I love you both.

February 20, 1943

I want pictures taken at least once a month of the baby and I
believe that, with some ingenuity, you can get really good ones.
I imagine it would be pretty trying but a little patience should put
it over. I'm being robbed of its first months, maybe years, and I
resent that very much. I believe pictures will make it very real and
very dear to me and I want some even if we have to hire a
photographer to take them.

We got 10 stalks of bananas yesterday and 600 ears of corn.
I got out and arranged for it. It sure peps the meal up for a bit of
a change. The corn is young horse feed but it didn't come out of
a can – and hadn't been dehydrated.

The candy from Jary is holding out mighty well although it
has proven to be almost too popular with everyone who comes
around my tent, especially Bill Laird. He divides everything he
gets with me, though, so I have little cause for complaint.

One of the boys got a letter from his wife the other day telling
him she was pregnant and asking him for a divorce so she could
marry the child's father. (I hope she knows who he is.) That sort
of thing isn't uncommon at all and it certainly doesn't help
morale any for the men to be reminded that their wives could be
playing around. Sabotage, I calls it!

The bugle just blew and I still have to address this so I'll
close hurriedly. Tell our families hello for me and remember how
much I love you.

February 21, 1943

I found two great big bundles waiting for me when I got home. A
five-pound package of "jaw breakers" from Jary that was really
welcome. In the first place, they are very good and, in the
second place, they'll last a long time – and that is of no little
importance now that we have been cut out of getting any more
packages. It was packed in a big tin box that should be of great
use to me, also. The other package was from a Mary Margaret
Imbt, 4218 Kenwood, Fort Worth, and contained 20 or more

handmade scrapbooks each filled with cartoons and crossword puzzles cut from the newspapers. Each one was bound with brightly colored yarn and very neatly made.

I don't need to tell you what I thought of them as you know what a sucker I am when somebody does something nice for my soldiers. It made quite a hit with the boys, as they are quick to realize when thought, time and effort have been spent on things for them and they value them accordingly.

It's funny too that I seem to have a great deal more physical desire for you now that I'm sure the baby has been born. For some time, I've felt what was, for me at least, a minimum of actual bodily desire but right now I feel as I'd feel if we were just starting on a honeymoon. A very nice feeling, I might add.

I'm not sure that you've ever really understood that my constant desire for you has been the nicest part of our life together to me. I can't conceive of anything any worse than being tied to a person whose attraction had failed and I think it is a wonderful tribute to you and to our marriage that your attraction has become greater and greater as time has passed. Especially since I can feel as I do now and still not waver in my loyalty to you.

They've invented radios that send their beam only in the direction of the receiving station for which it is intended and I guess that is the way my love and desire for you is hooked up. I know that our love will stand up through any crisis so long as we each know the other is loyal and faithful to it. And you can be sure that we'll never have enough children, enough misfortune or enough good luck to keep you yourself from being my prime consideration in life.

I don't know just what brings all this on right now but there are almost no mosquitoes tonight and my lantern is quite outdoing itself for a change, shining with a white, clear flame just like my love for you.

I had Kessler open the packages and he got a lot of fun out of it. He opens all my packages for me because I enjoy his eagerness. I guess my "kid" days are gone – the days I felt like model building and racing with trains, etc. – but I hope I never get too old or too saddled with responsibilities for enjoying young people or to begrudge them the pleasures that are peculiar only to youth. (Imagine me, turning philosopher!)

I might as well take my dreams of you and home and put them to bed – so, if you'll pardon me, I'll close. I love you.

February 23, 1943

I sometimes think that civilian life will be pretty uneventful after the way we've been living over here. We build buildings without lumber or nails, we keep flies out without screen, feed horses without hay, install floors without cement. Now the colonel wants us to get work done without labor. Every man has to go to training periods all day and still build mess halls and corrals. It is impossible, of course, and just forces us to be a bunch of sneaks. But, if that's the way he wants it, that's the way I want him to have it.

We are progressing nicely with our mess hall in spite of his attitude and it will be dearer to us thanks to his opposition. I've often wondered what many of the regular officers could do for a living in civilian life but I know just what he'd be suited for – he's such a good tearer-downer he should organize a house-wrecking company.

I am no longer in command of the squadron as they suddenly decided to close the camp where Rupert has been and he was necessarily returned here for duty. I hate it as I thought I was doing very well but will have more freedom now to rest and for my correspondence with you and the family.

I guess I'm in a bad humor tonight but if I am it is largely because I'm terribly and actively homesick. I don't let myself get this bad very often and will snap out of it pretty quickly. If we were unloading ships at the docks or digging badly needed ditches, it wouldn't be so bad – but it sometimes makes me flat sick at my stomach to stop and realize how little we do to further the war effort by being over here grooming a bunch of skinny, moth-eaten, second-rate Australian nags. We would be worth infinitely more at home guarding defense plants or even just working in them!

Well, now that I've got all that off my chest maybe I can settle down and write you a little more peacefully. The reason that I am homesick (I guess lonesome is a better word) is because I miss you so very badly. And, I suppose, because I resent not getting to see the new baby.

I'm really hurting because I am away from you and because I know so well what I'm missing in love and companionship and sheer physical delight by being separated from you for so long. I don't mind the discomforts that we put up with here and I long ago became reconciled to being exposed to the colonel's frenzies and senile tantrums. And I realize that I am not being imposed upon unduly by being in foreign service. I just, and only on rare occasions, allow myself to realize how much it really truly hurts me to be away from you. And when I do let myself go it is almost for the moment more than I can stand.

I know I shouldn't write all this and I believe I've been pretty cheerful in most of my letters – but I feel better already just for having written it down. And if you get from this the idea that I'm just a poor married guy who is terribly in love with his wife, then the whole thing will not have been in vain. I do love you and in no trivial sense of the word. Sweet thoughts of you are with me all day and much of the night, and when I get upset or unhappy over here, I draw on that love to bolster my courage just as one would draw money out of a bank. The only difference is that the love I have to draw upon is inexhaustible and is useful on many occasions where money in any quantity, however large an amount, would be of no value at all.

I often hear guys speak of what they're going to do the first night they are in San Francisco, and that seems to be the sort of thoughts that they use to console themselves for the present plight. But not me!! I plan weeks and months and years together with you – the two of us being happy together raising our family.

I'm going to close as I feel pretty happy right now and want to go to bed and dream of you because I love you.

February 26, 1943

I am a little confused about the baby as the Red Cross cable said "daughter" and Mama's letter of Feb. 6 says "son". I'm very curious now for sure as to whether we have a boy or a girl. Mama had not even seen it when she wrote her letter just after it had been born that morning. I feel sure I'll hear from you in a few days and I am sure you'll know whether it is a boy or a girl! V-mail seems to get through faster now, so be sure to use it for sending important information.

I received the pictures of Mama, Dad and the Christmas tree but none of you although they mentioned something about a picture of you. I sure want you to get a camera and take some as soon as you feel like it, as it really is fine when you open a letter and find them. How about some in a bathing suit?

Just remember that I love you.

February 28, 1943

I have that sort of "useless" feeling so peculiar to aimless Sunday nights. You remember how they used to be at Clark. I've laid around all afternoon reading (an unaccustomed luxury, lately) and now I don't want to go to bed – and, worse, can't think of anything else to do. Of course, I have one pastime that is almost invariably soothing – that is in spending my leisure moments thinking of you and, now, the baby, too. Incidentally, I got a V-mail from Mama written as soon as she found out that the "son" business was in error. As I told you the other day, I was almost certain that it was a daughter all along and wasn't particularly upset about the misinformation.

I'm finally getting the paternal feeling. Mama referred to me as "Dad" in her letter and it took a minute for it to soak in that she meant me. I feel sort of like I felt when I put on my first long pants! It's really wonderful.

Mama said you had a chance on the apartment after all and I hope you took it. I like the idea of you being near your mother a great deal and I think it will be unusually convenient for you. It's a long old streetcar ride from that far out on Travis to the Northside.

She mentioned pictures of the baby and I wish you would buy some film and get Hazel to take some at regular intervals. I think pictures will be a great help to me in keeping myself "adjusted" to it. Of course, I'm jealous as hell of you for having it all to yourself but I don't see how it can be helped, as it weighs over 5 lb and can't be mailed to me.

We have a line on a "walk-in" cooler for the squadron but I'm afraid to count on it as it's almost too good to be true. Imagine having a place to keep drinking water cold – or to make jello – or maybe even ice cream!! It looks like we can get fresh eggs for breakfast, too, although the flat price on the island is $1.00 per dozen. (Boy! Do we get rooked!!)

I miss you constantly and hope the baby will serve to keep you from being as lonely as I get at times. I love you.

March 3, 1943

I slipped off from drill this morning with a 2½-ton truck and 8-wheel trailer to bring our icebox out but it has rained so much that we couldn't get it. The thing weighs over 5,000 pounds and so there was no question of moving it to the truck. We will just have to be patient. It is burning the rest of the regiment up considerably because they don't know who is letting us have it.

Even the colonel has dropped hints that he would like to know where it is to come from – but no soap. One of the considerations in the deal was that we would not get a bunch of people worrying this man for boxes – and we mean to keep our part of the deal!

I don't know what project I'll start next but I try to keep something going all the time to keep me occupied. It's one way (I hope) to keep from going nuts.

The baby is gradually becoming a distinct personality in my mind as I get more information about her. I also know that I'll be able to visualize her even more as a separate entity after I find out her name. I love you both.

March 5, 1943

I won't get to sleep any tomorrow afternoon as I am on a Grand Court Martial downtown. The guy that notified me seemed to think it would be a pretty interesting session – of course, he could not tell me what it was but said it was "different". Some soldier must have raped a mule as we have tried at least one case of every other kind!

I got two letters from Dad yesterday both raving about you and the baby. If he is disappointed in our having a girl, I don't believe he could have stood the strain of a boy! He's really thrilled and they've decided now that it looks like Hazel. The poor kid will have looked like everybody on both sides of the family before it is 10 days old!

I know she is one month old tomorrow but she is just two days old to me as that is the most recent word I've had. I've seen huge clocks, the minute hands of which moved in visible jerks rather than in a smooth even sweep as on normal clocks and that is the way time passes for me – each letter represents a jerk and, of course, my "time clock" stays four to six weeks behind.

Just remember I love you.

March 7, 1943

It is before 7:00 a.m. and I am having to write this seated on my deck chair on my "front porch" because it is still too dark for me to see in my tent.

I awakened at 6:00 (0600, we call it) but reveille isn't blown until 0700 on Sunday and I have a little spare time. I have had coffee, toast, butter and jelly already and thought I'd get this started. Who knows, I might get time to write you two letters in one day – that would really be a luxury for me.

I got a letter from Mama and one from Hazel Friday both dated February 1st and both very encouraging as to your condition. Of course, I know the baby has been born and I've been assured that both of you are doing well, but I lap up any reference to you in my mail no matter how old the news is.

I got a V-mail from Dad last night but don't know when he mailed it, as it wasn't dated. However, he mentioned having to look at the baby through glass and I presume it is still in the hospital. He also referred to it as Virginia Gayle but said that name was tentative. As I've said before, I think naming the baby after you is swell. I haven't insisted on any particular name because I want you to name it whatever you like the best. All of your suggested names have been very good, I think, and I liked Laura Louise as well as any although I can't say I liked it any better than Virginia Gayle.

So far as I can see now, V-mail is getting a decided lead on air mail for speed in transmission as all the "baby news" I have had has been from Mama and Dad by V-mail. Here's my idea of how to whip V-mail and you can see what you think of it. I have always wanted a portable typewriter and I suggest you try to buy a good one. Underwood puts out a really good one called the Nationally Advertised "Underwood Streamlined". They are in color, I think, and have many excellent features. You'll have to buy a second hand one but I think, with your practical knowledge, you could pick up a good one. That is the only way you can get a whole letter on one sheet of V-mail and it will also help you keep yourself up to date on typing. I started to buy myself one two or three times at Clark and I really wish I had now. At any rate, I plan on one after the war.

I have so little insurance that I especially like the idea of your keeping fresh on your typing. I'm not remotely worried about anything happening to me (of course, I could die of sheer boredom), but it is foolish not to recognize that anything is possible.

We finally got our refrigerator and it's really a good one, a 150 cu. ft. box with a 4-cycle motor as motor power. The regiment is green with envy. We should have it in operation by Tuesday at the latest and that will really be "something"!

It rains continually here. Everything is soggy and our clothing and leather require constant attention as mildew pops out in nothing flat. I just go ahead and stay wet all the time as a raincoat is a minimum of protection and a maximum of nuisance.

We have been issued our service bars for having been into the service prior to 1943 and also our bar for serving in the Asiatic Pacific Theater. We should get our Guadalcanal citation bars pretty soon as we were sent here and held in reserve as part of the Solomon action. I'm sure we came mighty close to moving up for a little more active participation more times than we'll ever realize. None of us wear the ribbons anyhow but they'll make nice trinkets for the baby some day, maybe.

I guess the baby suits everybody from the way Dad sounds. If all your family thinks it looks like the Dickersons and all of mine think it looks like the Hunnicutts, then everything is lovely. That would make it the perfect child!! I hope it looks like you and I'm sure that it will – to me, anyhow.

Keep yourself young and happy. I love you both very much.

March 8, 1943

I got your V-mail late yesterday dated Feb. 14 (#72) and got a tremendous kick out of it as it was my first from you that has been written since the baby was born. I am naturally pleased that the baby is named after you and I only hope that it will be just like you in many other ways.

I am glad you enjoyed the red roses and I'm sure you realize how much I enjoyed arranging for them to be sent. That's about over, though, as I'll be destitute now that I've signed up for the extra $50 bond for Gayle each month. I can still afford stamps, however, and will keep on writing to you!!

We started our icebox this afternoon and ran the engine for an hour or so to break it in. We didn't hook it to the compressor, however, because we didn't want to run it at night under a load. We'll start it again tomorrow morning with a mechanic there to watch it for us and, if it runs OK all day, we will leave it on automatic operation tomorrow night. There is always a chance of burning a bearing and I just won't take the chance. Overcautious, I suppose, but the only times I've ever been in a jam were times when I wasn't cautious enough. Old Maid Hunnicutt!

If I am discharged at the end of 18 months, we could have around $4,000 saved. Of course, I realize that you may not be able to save that much – but I am setting that as a goal and we may be able to come close to it. The main reason that I set any goal at all is that it makes me feel more secure about you over here and also it makes me feel a little better about having to be away so long. (I really want security.)

There can't help but be a tremendous economic depression eventually, say ten or fifteen years, after the war, just when we'll be most anxious for our baby to have a good home and nice friends and my haphazard, "everything-will-be-alright" days are over so far as I'm concerned. I realize that I'll come home and take whatever kind of job I can get and start in much as I did before. I'll have to start new at 35 or 36 years of age and the odds will be against me. But I'm not afraid of it at all except for the disappointments I may have whenever I have to deny either of you anything you may want.

It gets a little rough on me out here every now and then when I realize how long it is since I last saw you – and how long it may be before I get to see you again. I love you.

March 10, 1943

We threw the whole load on our icebox this morning and it is already down below 50° and going on down pretty fast. I have 6 bottles of New Zealand beer and I just put it in for supper – if somebody doesn't beat us to it. I guess it is safe, though, as Tommie Driggers has the keys to the box.

The most recent news we've gotten here is pretty encouraging although lots of it hasn't been announced as yet. I still think we will be gone at least 16 to 18 more months unless we are among the fortunate few who are sent home for duty or because of sickness or insanity.

I just got a letter from Mama dated Feb. 10th, so I guess V-mail isn't always faster than airmail. (This was airmail.) She raved about the baby and you and all the lovely gifts it has received. She also enclosed a clipping announcing the baby that I'll send back to you for the baby book.

I want you to keep the book up because that will be all of its first year or two that I will ever have and I want to keep everything we can. I hate being away from it badly and hope we can have another some day that I can help rear. I miss you constantly and spend all my spare time sweating the mail line. Write soon and remember that I love you both very much.

March 13, 1943

The icebox is running beautifully and Tommie and I made up a batch of canned milk, water, vanilla and sugar and got it cold last night. We drank it after the picture show and it was so cold that I had a stomach ache for an hour but it tasted so good that I plan on having a stomach ache just like it every day.

I keep feeling like we will be moved one of these days though I don't expect anything sudden. Keeping us here seems stupid, but that is just my opinion. We could stay here another year just as easily. I've lost a lot of my respect for cavalry as an ordinary branch and believe uses for it will be unusual. We need to either go fight or come home and turn ourselves into something else.

If I were running things, I'd send this outfit home and make three tank-destroyer battalions out of it – but, as I am often reminded, I am not running things, so we will probably have to stay here and groom for the duration. It's safe enough, of course, for a person with enough self-control to refrain from suicide.

I got a letter from your mother. I sop up all references to the baby like a camel taking on water so don't be afraid of boring me. I miss you constantly and would paddle home in a native outrigger if they'd just give me a chance. It's a good thing the trip can't be made on horseback! I love you.

March 17, 1943

As you know, I am not much inclined to use a typewriter for personal correspondence but my sleeves are wet and I don't think I could use a pen without smearing the paper and I can't roll my sleeves up because of the mosquitoes. I have to write, though, because I got the letter you wrote just after the baby came (No. 71) and the pictures as well.

Needless to say, I got a lot of pleasure out of your letter and really appreciated it since I was so sure the writing of it cost you a tremendous effort. The pictures were grand and really give me a chance to feel like we actually had a child instead of just feeling like I was reading about a fictional baby that would disappear at the end of each letter.

I am mighty proud of the baby pictures and, of course, they only whetted my appetite for more. It has been a little hard to realize that it was really true, but I am finally becoming convinced. I suppose it has been harder for me than for Phil because we have wanted children such a long, long time. Your letters (and the letters from home, also) have gone a long way to make the baby a reality to me and I get lots of pleasure out of sitting around and planning her future.

Everyone in the regiment is disgusted in every way. Not only is the weather quite aggravating, but the colonel gets harder to serve under and many of the officers are looking frantically for some place to go to besides here. As all the units on the island are anxious for experienced officers, I am afraid we are due to take some bad losses that will weaken us considerably. I don't get excited so much myself for several reasons. In the first place, he doesn't get on me about anything to speak of and, in the second place, I learned a long time ago that nothing is static and that time will correct almost any condition (or replace it with something worse!) Most of the older of us have considerably more patience, but the younger officers who haven't had their ears so thoroughly beaten down are fast reaching saturation point.

Of course, the real, basic trouble lies in the fact that someone somewhere made the colossal mistake of sending cavalry into a combat area that is primarily naval in character and apparently either doesn't realize their mistake or else won't admit it. I don't think there is 10 square miles of cavalry country in the entire SW Pacific area and none of us can see any sense in putting up with the discomforts of our life here or the various standard unpleasantnesses of the regiment when it is all wasted anyhow. We've had lots of fusses and quarrels in the past two and a half years but all of us remained at least loyal to the regiment itself and it worries me now because most of the officers don't even have loyalty to the regiment any more.

So far as I can see, the greatest trouble that we have is the fact that the colonel complains of our lack of initiative and then literally insults anyone who has the temerity to use their own judgment for even the simplest of objectives. He has never at any time indicated that he thought any of us had enough sense to come in out of the rain and, if we ever demonstrated it by actually coming in out of the rain, he'd tear us to pieces and send us back out without our raincoats.

It doesn't help us any, now that we are stuck off in the wilds, to look back and realize how expertly he beat us out of our leaves of absence and worked us on our own time on Wednesday afternoons, Saturday afternoons and Sundays, when we were entitled to rest occasionally. No one would complain if there was any purpose in it, but we are, in the general opinion, a total loss over here, although the colonel gives us every reason to believe that he has visions of us making mounted attacks in parade-ground formations against a presumably hypnotized foe who, for some reason or other, doesn't have sense enough to load a machine gun and wipe us out in their spare time. Well, I could go on like this for hours – I could hire Carnegie Hall and entertain the General Staff for at least two hours without repetition, if I thought it would do any good.

We have received a hurricane warning for tonight and have tried to tie everything possible securely. We are in a very well-sheltered location and I don't expect our squadron to have a great deal of trouble, even if we get a pretty high wind. Most of them blow themselves out at sea.

It is beginning to blow a little and I'd better close and check up on our "anti-wind" arrangements. Write soon and remember that I love you.

March 21, 1943

We have really had a tremendous rain complete with a nice little flood all our own. The hurricane that I mentioned the other night passed us by, but we apparently got the squalls from the edges of it and it rained for two nights and a day as hard or harder than I have ever seen it rain in my life. The streams are so short and the ground around here so precipitous that they overflow all over the little narrow valleys between the watersheds. We were cut off from our stable areas by a little stream in which we normally water our horses for over 24 hours except for a water main and a narrow footbridge, either one of which required a pretty good sense of balance to cross. Of course, we live in "balconies" hung on the sides of the hills and our tents, for the most part, were reasonably dry.

I feel pretty damned good tonight as I am sitting in our new mess hall out of the mosquitoes writing this letter and am pretty happy to see it satisfactorily completed. We have had to overcome literally tremendous difficulties to get it built and I am quite proud of it. It is about the size of our living room at Fort Clark, not counting the kitchen, and we have three large tables, each covered with very gay oilcloth (at $1.00 per yard).

We are having our first breakfast in the morning and the boys are mixing the pancakes now and putting the finishing touches on everything in general.

I went to town Saturday morning with Tommie and bought the oilcloth, a few extras in the food line and arranged for a couple of loads of scrap lumber to make our benches. We've built the whole thing out of logs, mud and grass, except for cement for the floor and screen for the windows. It sounds pretty silly to let such a thing seem so important, I know, but we have so very little to draw pleasure from that I hope you will be tolerant if I write too much about it.

Tommie and I keep a gallon jug of milkshake, made from condensed milk, in the icebox 24 hours a day. I drink a big batch about 11 every morning after drill, again about 3 in the afternoon, and then before I go to bed. I feel sure it will be good for me and I really truly enjoy it.

I had three letters from Mama yesterday, all being regular air mail and written just after the baby came. I got an unusually big kick out of them, especially since she went to so much trouble to describe the baby, you, and her visits to see you both. Also, she devoted a letter to the apartment, which made it sound pretty keen. Since I had the pictures that had already been sent, I was able to get a pretty good idea of the whole thing. She even drew floor plans!

You'd be surprised how much we see in pictures – the wallpaper, the pattern of the upholstery, the chrome lamp on the table that used to sit on my desk at Clark. I really drink it all in and you can't overestimate their value so far as I am concerned.

The boys are frying off some sample hotcakes and canned bacon for a little "surprise" snack. Kessler came down and volunteered to help them and just said "hello" for you. He is almost as proud of the baby as I am and has shown her pictures everywhere. I ought to transfer him some place where he has a chance at promotion but I hate to part with him.

I took quite a few pictures of the mess before it was completed but can't take any more as photography has been banned on the island. Sort of a silly rule, I think, coming this late.

I hope I can get my old letter-writing stride back again. (I wrote a letter to the baby for her book the other day but it sounded pretty silly so I tore it up.) Be sweet and happy – remember always that I love you both.

March 28, 1943

Another month, I notice, is about gone and it will soon have been nine months since I waved goodbye to you from the steps of the only train that I ever failed to enjoy riding. It seems like a lifetime has passed since then and I have certainly increased my conception of how much pain and lonesomeness a human being can endure.

Fortunately, I have learned to relegate my hurt at our separation to the very back of my consciousness for the most part, but I have certainly failed to reduce its intensity at all.

I am certain that we are luckier than most since we have such a lovely daughter and all of us are well and in as happy surroundings as the situation permits.

And, speaking of surroundings, I don't believe I have told you about my new tent that was started yesterday morning. One of Bill's QM friends gave us a load of truck crates and we are going to have tent frames made of the lumber. Mine is about half finished and will be really palatial in comparison to the gypsy tent I am living in now.

I read all of the news in most of my letters to Kessler and he seems to enjoy it. He's the only person over here who I am ready to admit is lonelier than I am! He takes it like a little man, though.

It seems funny that you can all write so much about Junior and I can write so little. You have me at a disadvantage in that you have her there with you and have lots to tell. I enjoy every word I hear about her and hope you don't mistake the little I can say for lack of interest. No one could be any prouder than I am nor any happier about her. I have all kinds of plans for her future – but it's a long time off, I suppose, and we can talk about that later.

In the meantime, I want you to remember that my thoughts are constantly of you both. I love you.

March 30, 1943

I sat out in a driving rain last night to see Bette Davis in *Now, Voyager* and came back to my tent at 10 o'clock to sit down and write you a letter. I was so thoroughly drenched and chilled that I decided to undress, dry myself and put on dry underwear so I could go to bed and warm up a little.

I hope you have seen the picture as it certainly made my heart ache for you. It concerns two people who love one another but are forced to live apart by circumstance. The kind of love that they possess for one another is the kind of love I have for you when I tell so often that I could live with you more happily "without" than I could with any other woman on earth "with".

The colonel's letter recommending Rupert's return to the US as being physically unfit came back disapproved today. However, I understand he is going to take the letter to Headquarters personally and push it through. At least, that is what he is supposed to have told Rupert today. I still feel Rupert is not long with us as the colonel positively told him he didn't think he was in condition to handle the squadron in combat and it would be pretty hard for him to back out. (The funniest things can happen in this outfit, can't they?)

I just this minute received some mail – a V-mail from Mama and another from Dad and airmail from Mama. Dad raves about the baby to the exclusion of all other subjects – doesn't mention weather, business, rationing or anything. As a result of your enthusiasm in the letters all of you write, I'm getting quite a thrill out of my fatherhood. They are all genuinely foolish about you and I can't help but be pleased that they approve of you so heartily since I love you so very much.

April 1, 1943

It may be that you won't be able to write as often now on account of Gayle. If not, I'll miss the letters but you can be sure that I will understand. I'm sure we agree that she will come first from now on in everything, as I feel sure our happiness together will largely be drawn from her in the future. I think it will be wonderful to watch her grow and develop and I know we will be able to take an enormous pride in her in the years to come.

To me, it seems that the more we love her, the more we will love one another. We have much to gain and nothing at all to lose. I am sure we would have been happy together all our lives without her, but I can't help but believe we will be even happier with her.

I saw *Random Harvest* last night and, of course, it was a wonderful picture. Since we have been separated, I have gotten the habit of putting us into the parts in most pictures. It isn't a conscious thing with me exactly, but I find myself more and more feeling that it is not an actor and an actress who go through the empty motions of love on the screen but that it is actually you and me. I guess the whole thing is sort of silly.

I came home to my tent after the movie and felt almost as though I had just had a short but happy visit with you. It was quite exhilarating and I am learning to look forward to picture shows with more anticipation. Of course, if I ever see one where a wife shoots her husband, I may drop dead before I realize better – but that is just a small risk to run in return for so much pleasure so I'll gladly take the chance! I love you.

April 8, 1943 – V-mail

I haven't done very well with my letter writing this week, as I have been moving into my new tent frame. The tent frame with screen on it and a concrete floor is luxury personified and I am really happy about it. Of course, you can't keep the mosquitoes out completely but it does give you a chance to corner them and fight them on even terms – they can't fly just out of reach and laugh at you like they could in an open tent!

Well, I'll have to close and try to get some sleep. Bedtime is the worst hour of the day for me and I stall it for as long as I possibly can. We will be able to make it up later. I love you.

April 11, 1943

This has been a big day for me. I got a real fistful of mail – three V-mails from you, three from Dad, one airmail from Hazel, and an airmail and two V-mails from Mama. As they were devoted to my darling daughter, I didn't get a great deal of news about anything else.

I have been feeling very well lately, but, of course, I couldn't feel good enough to make being away from you worthwhile. There are times when I suffer all the tortures of the damned when I let myself realize how much I miss you. It is pure yearning to be with you; to eat with you; sleep with you; tell you my troubles; and fuss at you and have you fuss at me. I'm saving myself for you and you had sure better need me when I get there!

I just exist from one letter to another so write often and remember that I think of you often and love you constantly.

April 14, 1943

Rupert really got slapped in the face today. The colonel put Grant in for promotion but not Rupert. As lousy a trick as I've run across in a long time. I never heard of a man being good enough to handle a job and still not being good enough to hold the rank that goes with it. I guess it is none of my business but it burns me up nevertheless.

Every letter from the folks has more detail – more praise, to be exact – concerning our offspring. I really feel sorry for other people who have just ordinary children.

I have hopes of some day walking into a nice place and asking if supper is ready. I know it will undoubtedly be a long time off, but some of the nicest things in my life have been almost completely unexpected.

For instance, I had been wanting to marry you for some time – and, all of a sudden, there we were, all married. So, if miracles can happen once, then they can happen twice. That belief is the only thing that really keeps me pushing down the road day after day. If I couldn't keep hoping for a break, then I'd lose the little courage that I am able to muster.

My horse has turned into a perfect baby and is gentle as a dog although he can still shake himself around a little on a cool morning. He is awfully nervous but quite dependable.

I'm writing this on an Australian typewriter that we picked up somewhere. It is an old, high-backed Remington and looks like the console of the Worth Theater organ – and is almost as hard to play. It has been dropped at some time or another in its career and the arm for spacing has been so badly bent that it will not work. When you punch the back spacer it skips from one to ten spaces in one direction or the other but never in the same direction twice. I'd rather make a parachute jump than mess with this typewriting monstrosity ever again. Write soon. I love you.

April 21, 1943

Well, just got back from seeing Errol Flynn in *Gentleman Jim* and it appears I owe an apology to the entire motion picture industry. It was an outstanding picture in every respect: casting, direction, photography and all. I really, truly got a keener enjoyment from it than from any picture I've seen in a long time.

I guess after all these years that I am really becoming a picture show fan. I probably would have been sooner except that there were lots of times when I was going to school when I didn't have the buck required to take a date to the show and I kidded everyone that I didn't like shows until I finally believed it myself. I guess pride has colored a lot of my other reactions, too, but I hope that I've had enough solitude over here to look back and realize how silly I've been lots of times.

We've had cross words when I knew I was wrong and wouldn't say so. None of them was really lastingly serious, I suppose, but I regret every unkind word that I have ever said to you and every unkind gesture.

There was a time, maybe, when I was a little afraid of my capacity for love, I think. I had jumped around from one girl to another so often and had been so fickle by nature that I was afraid I wasn't capable of the kind of love you read about in books. I realize now that I just didn't know anything about that kind of love – the kind of love I mean when I write "I love you" at the close of my letters to you.

I don't know what has brought all this on, but I guess a guy can write a love letter to his wife if he wants to, can't he? It must be respectable for me to do so – after all we have Gayle for a chaperone!

If I thought they would classify me as crazy and send me home, I'd paint myself up like an Indian and run around waving my hatchet and shrieking at the top of my voice, patting my mouth with the palm of my hand to secure the proper sound effect. I might even do a little scalping here and there. You can imagine where I'd start!

I don't have any idea of where you have moved nor of how you like it. I'm sure the dope is en route to me – I wish this dope (me – get it?) was en route to you – and I am naturally anxious to hear.

I hate to quit, baby, because I want to keep on and on just writing one little phrase – I love you.

April 25, 1943

If I were a mystic, I am sure that I would tie up an experience I had in a dream last night with the fact that this is actually Easter Sunday. Since I am not, and since I dream of you often (last night's dream was just more vivid than usual), I'll just say that I was (or am) a very fortunate young man to have such a pleasant subject for my dreams.

More and more, as time passes, do I seem able to concentrate my subconscious mind upon you and the result is quite enjoyable. I often awaken to feel that I have just been with you – and to have a little of that happy glow with which I know I will be suffused when I am finally with you again.

I suppose it is all a mental "defense mechanism" of some sort, but it actually seems that, from time to time, when I seem to have gone as long as I can go without you, I have these dreams of you.

I can't tell you how pleasant the "visits" with you are. I can go for several days at a time with a sort of exhilarated feeling that I have just seen you or am just going to see you soon. And, although the physical relief that I get from them is purely abstract, the mental relief that I receive from these ethereal meetings with you is quite concrete in every way.

I think I am realizing for the first time the full import of those phrases in the marriage ceremony about "in sickness and in health," etc., because I know now, as I never knew before, that nothing will ever be able to separate us. Our life together must have been foreordained since the Creation and, to me, it is as inevitable as Death. I could no more fail to come home to you than I could imagine a moth failing to be drawn to the most intense light within its horizons. I know that you can never be fat enough or ugly enough or sick enough or mean enough for me to be happy away from you.

The fact that I am so completely true to you every hour of the day or night and so devoted to you in my every thought makes me believe implicitly in your fidelity to me. I think I would literally lose my mind if I ever had any doubts of you over here. But my love for you is strong enough to assure me that you will not be tempted and that you will be as true and honest with me as I am with you.

There is nothing in the world as reassuring as love and nothing that is freer. It comes unasked and stays and grows upon you without any effort of your own: a sort of catalytic agent that operates to change two humans and fuse them together without the love itself becoming changed or losing any of its force. There are often by-products to any chemical reaction and I suppose, to carry a poor simile to its logical (?) completion, that Gayle is a product of our fusion, a concrete proof that our love is as good and clean and true as I have always thought it. Somehow, I get a real pleasure from thinking that because we are in love our children and our children's children will be able to live and love for countless generations to come. The fact that our love has made this possible would justify it alone, not even considering our pleasures from it.

You never have mentioned censorship at all and I am curious to know whether any of my letters have been opened. It doesn't really make any difference, as I don't think I've been putting out any hot dope. As a matter of fact, I'd have a hard time helping the Japs with information if I were actually trying as we never hear anything except "Mount" and "Dismount"! I'm not even sure the high command remembers we are here.

I can't begin to tell you of the peaceful pleasure that I get from my new screened-in tent. It is practically mosquito-proof and I haven't used a net since I moved in. I have the net fastened from two parallel wires drawn taut above the bed. It is suspended by safety pins from the wires like a shower curtain and I can slide it out over the bed or push it back against the wall in about two seconds flat. I almost regret not needing it, it is so cleverly arranged.

I have to go now and inspect some horse as surveying officer "with a view to condemnation". I have little time for sentiment, it seems, and have to make each spare moment count to the fullest. I'm not going to read this letter over – it's probably too silly to mail. I'll just say – I love you.

May 1, 1943

I went to the dance tonight for about an hour. I can still shoot a wicked line of baloney at a bull session, so managed to enjoy myself. But, baby, if preferring to come home and write to your wife on such dry subjects instead of dancing is true love, then I've got it bad! I carried the good picture of you and Gayle with me tonight to the dance and showed it to everyone. I hate people who go around showing pictures, but I go right on showing mine just the same. I think I'll paste it inside my helmet!

I think Gayle has made Dad about 20 years younger. He has become the best correspondent I've ever had and starts each letter by saying "Well, boy, I went out to see my granddaughter yesterday…!" He really pours it on (and I really eat it up).

I truly think that my chances of coming home will be greatly improved in the next few months and feel sure I'll make it before the end of the year at the latest. Chances here have been negligible and rightly so, I think. We can only hope. I love you.

May 3, 1943

I often wonder as I write "Dearest Virginia" time and again why I never refer to you as "Dearest Wife" or "Dearest Sweetheart". The only substitute I could possibly think up would be "Dearest Everything". You are not in my mind as just a wife or just a sweetheart or just as any one thing to me. I like to think of us as a lovely ring with you as the jewel and me as the utilitarian part that supports you and holds you tightly in my fingers safely and securely so that all the world may see and admire but none can take you from me. And there are so many facets to my jewel – as a wife, mother, sweetheart, dancing date, lover and mistress (I could have added cook, housekeeper, laundress, I guess) – that I can't refer to you as any one of them. Instead I just say Virginia and that covers the whole thing.

I almost forgot to tell you how proud the 10-week report on Gayle made me but I knew you'd take care of our baby long before we ever even thought we could have one. I love you.

May 10, 1943 – V-mail

I think I had one of the loveliest experiences of my life last night and I want to tell you about it early today before I do anything else and while it is still fresh on my mind. I had the most realistic dream of you that I can imagine. We were together somewhere with no worries of war or separation and it could not have been more complete or satisfactory if we had actually been together.

Unless you have had the same experience, you can't imagine the feeling I have this morning of your nearness to me. I realize that you are not right here with me now but it seems as though I had but to call out and you would appear by my side.

It is really a lovely feeling and I wouldn't swap it for a ten-day leave – unless I could actually see you. I hate to go to breakfast or mix in any way with the others this morning because I know that it will start to wear away and I want to save all of it I can for as long as I can.

If I had such a dream as a reward for my good behavior while I have been here, I can only say that I have been well paid and I would be only too glad to trade another extended period of abstinence for another dream just half so sweet as this one was.

It's time to go to work now, baby, and this isn't much of a letter – but any letter is good when I can say – I love you.

May 10, 1943

I haven't received the photos nor pictures that you sent April 14th and 20th but feel sure I will by Wednesday or Thursday which will be OK. I have the picture of you and Gayle cut down to fit my billfold and will have it handy from now on to illustrate my lectures on how to raise babies!

That's all for now. I love you.

May 16, 1943

I am going to leave the 1943 off all my letters from now on. After all, I don't intend to be far away any other year to need to write you letters so there shouldn't be any confusion.

You may have suspected that we were preparing to move; if so, you were exactly right. We are on a transport now. I wrote Dad a letter for his birthday and gave the details of the trip. I am sure he will read it to you and won't go into details except to say that this ship should be named the USS *Glide* (which is certainly not its name). It is the smoothest sailing ship you can imagine and it is hard to remember you are at sea.

We have commodious cabins, lovely meals and the ship's officers are very pleasant and give us welcome changes in our associates. Altogether, it has been a lovely trip and my only regret is that it is not peacetime and you and Gayle are not with me.

I received the two letters with the snapshots the day I came aboard and am really pleased with them. They were really good pictures and Kessler got a kick out of the fact that Gayle was wearing his gifts.

I feel like a million. I am at my best at sea and would ask nothing better than to spend the rest of my enforced stay from home on a transport. I certainly plan for us to have a good trip somewhere as soon as I get out of this mess. I love you.

May 19, 1943

Here I am "somewhere in Australia". Imagine your surprise! We are hopelessly entangled in dust, work and the British monetary system. The money is a conglomerate mess of pounds, quids, bobs, shillings, pence, ha' pence, etc. that is almost as interesting as a picture puzzle – and about as hard to unravel.

The best part of my crossing consisted of my daily trip to the top of the forecastle head to watch the sunset. The Bos'n's Mate (a chief petty officer) stood watch there during the early morning and late evening "General Quarters" period (the most dangerous periods aboard ship begin an hour before sunrise and sunset and last until an hour after each) and I was sort of a guest.

I was on the bridge when we sailed into port and I really got a big kick out of it as we passed the vessels at anchor. They were of all descriptions although most of them, of course, were naval vessels of one kind or another. Battleships don't look so big when you're on the bridge of a pretty big liner yourself although I must confess that "flat tops" (aircraft carriers) still overawe me a bit. I suppose it is because they are built up so high in addition to being both long and wide. We unloaded our own ship this time and did in one day what it took over five days for the stevedores to do before.

Although our camp area here is not much, if any, better than we had on our second fiasco at Bliss and the dust is pretty bad, it is still nice to be in an English-speaking community where you ask for the things you want to buy or ask directions when you get lost. It is a little hard for us to understand the natives (white Australians, I mean), but we are learning. They talk so fast and have different pronunciations for some of their words and, of course, they have a twang to their talk that we are not accustomed to hear.

Our food here is very good as this seems to be the season for fresh vegetables and we are getting lots of them: sweet potatoes, cucumbers and cabbage in profusion. We even had sliced tomatoes for supper. We get 500 pounds of dressed beef per 100 men each week which is a reasonably generous allowance, especially when you consider that we get an additional 100 pounds of pork. We also get quite a little fresh fruit including apples, oranges and bananas. We have had pineapple twice in the two days we've been here and they are gigantic in size compared to those at our last station. They look like small nail kegs with a fern growing out of them!

It is a lovely night here with the full moon shining down out of a sky made of pale blue satin. It is one of those nights that make our separation especially difficult and I hope that sleep will come in a hurry to ease my pain.

I am going to send Gayle a cable tomorrow. It is really for you but I thought I would make a nice memento for her baby book. My new APO is 712, so use it often and remember that I love you.

May 22, 1943

I was able to get a commercial cable off to you all this morning and addressed it to Gayle so as to be completely impartial. I got quite a kick out of sending her the first greetings of any kind she has ever had from me and will have to admit that I'm sissy enough to feel a little choked up about it. You see she has finally become a very definite personality to me, just as much so as any of the rest of you are, and, so, I miss her, in a way, as much as I miss everyone else.

We put in a full day now at hard work and I am tired enough to be able to sleep beautifully when night finally comes. I am in excellent physical condition and the 12 miles we knock off every morning doesn't remotely faze me – not even when we carry our combat packs which weigh 51 lb. It does tire us, though, and I can always use the 9–11 hours sleep I get every night.

We almost have a mutiny every time we force the men to turn out for volleyball or indoor baseball, as they want to use any free time for resting or doing their laundry. It makes it a little hard on us, too, as we are inclined to agree with them. Nevertheless, we turned them out and played the games. I played catch with Jeffress and a couple of the boys for about 30 minutes, but noticed about ten guys sitting around and organized a game of "one-and-over", a form of leap frog. I played with them so they couldn't quit and you can imagine how tired and sore I am now. I am sure that I haven't played since I left junior high 19 years ago. I did very well, though, for a guy of 34.

The heat here around noon is terrific. I think it is hotter than Clark would be in July or August. However, it cools quickly in the late afternoon and I sleep under three blankets at night and shiver at the breakfast table every morning. If we keep this up long, they will have to "dilute" us as we'll be too tough for the Japs entirely.

If there was ever an outfit ready to fight, this one is. And, if we get into things, we'll make the Marines look like a kindergarten class.

I'd better try to get some sleep. Remember that I love you always.

May 26, 1943

Believe it or not, I wandered over to the squadron orderly tent after supper and got myself involved in a volleyball game with the boys. I played for over an hour which will give you an idea of what a good condition I am in, since it was after a pretty tiring day. And, what's more, I really enjoyed it!

Rupert came back from the hospital today and doesn't look at all well. However, my guess is that he intends to remain frail from now on, so I suppose I might as well get used to it! I don't blame him a great deal as he really isn't strong enough for the things we do. Also, I think he is too old to build up to it as the rest of us seem to be able to do.

Our new medico, a Captain Cathie, is a dyed-in-the-wool Scotsman, complete with the burr in his voice. He is a "muckle onhoppy mon" when things go wrong. His manner of speech isn't an affectation at all and we like him and enjoy him a great deal. He hasn't missed a march, either, although he has not been in the service very long and this is his first time with a line outfit so far as I know.

I love you.

May 28, 1943

I received a suit of silk underwear from Dad as a birthday gift. It is really nice and I'll put it aside for my homecoming trousseau. Can you imagine a guy going out Jap-stalking in silk underwear? That would be just too, too much! I am tempted to wear it as I love silk underwear (thoughtful of Dad to remember, wasn't it?) but think I'll just keep it as a gentle reminder of the civilized life that awaits me some fine day. I still have the Old Spice that Margaret sent and just use it on rare occasions for that "lift" that I don't always get from Camels.

I was able to get Gayle a gorgeous opal yesterday which I will mail home within a few days. I would like for you to have it made up into a necklace for her. It is about an inch long and is white and pear-shaped – teardrop, I believe it is called. The colors are more subdued than in the fire opals but I thought it would be lovely with a baby's skin and it was more expensive than the others. I am including a two-carat square-cut sapphire for you and I want it made into a dinner ring with, possibly, a small diamond on each side.

I know you'll love the opal for Gayle as it is truly beautiful, no fooling. Rupert and I got the last two "double" opals although there was quite a bit of the "single" stuff. "Singles" are flat and thin and have to be backed up by a plastic back to give them strength. They are quite cheap and I may get one later for a tiepin.

It is hard for me to destroy my mail as I get it but I do it every day it comes. I am sure you can understand why we can't let it stack up and that we can't have any identifying junk around if, as, and when we move on from here. I can keep the pictures and you must not write anything on them to identify my organization if I am to do so. I can't imagine that you will, of course, but want to be sure. Military rules must be obeyed.

I really hurt at times from wanting to be with you and Gayle and I miss you more every day (and every night). I love you.

May 30, 1943

I want to tell you that Ed Berry received your and Gayle's picture yesterday which had been sent to him by his mother who, I presume, received it from her relatives there in Fort Worth; it is odd that I should receive the picture by such a roundabout route on the day following your letter telling me it was to be in the paper. It was quite gratifying, particularly since it was such a very good picture of you both. I was (and am) quite proud of it and have done everything except post it on the bulletin board for all to see.

Of course, I can't tell just who Gayle looks like except Gayle, but I do believe she has my ears! It is a good picture. She looks as fat as a butterball.

The censorship rules here seem to be stricter than we have been accustomed to having heretofore and it sort of interferes with my writing as I am always afraid of saying something objectionable although I am dead sure that I don't know anything that would even remotely interest the "Mata Hari-est" spy that ever lived.

We have had inspection now and it is almost noon. We were inspected by the same person who used to inspect us at Clark. He is still as particular as ever and expressed himself as being highly pleased with nearly everything. You mentioned that we might run across him in one of your letters a month or so ago – and sure enough, we did! Quite a few officers of other units were brought down to inspect our kitchens this morning and also to see B troop do the manual of arms. Naturally, this made us feel pretty good.

I love you constantly and never forget for a moment that I am all yours and yours alone. You can count on me all the way and be sure of that. No anticlimaxes for me! I love you both.

June 7, 1943

I have received six more letters, all of them airmail. They included one from you, three letters from Mama, and two from Dad.

You'll never know how anxiously I awaited news of her arrival! You had been so very anxious for her for so many years and I was so afraid that you might miscarry and be deprived of her. I never dared mention such a thing, of course, and am terribly happy that she is strong and healthy.

I have always been a mental "jack-of-all-trades" and suppose I will be even more so after the war. I'll be amphibious, ambidextrous and a few other things if we stay over here much longer. There's nothing the marines can do that we cannot do better unless it is getting publicity.

The colonel informed us just last week that this was a good outfit but only because he had made it one! Well, everybody to their own opinion. I'm sort of like the tramp who said, "Well, if you're so damned smart, why aren't you rich?"

It's time to go out for a little night training so I'll have to close. We are literally becoming "sons of the beaches" and I almost have to sprinkle sand in my sheets to sleep – or would have to if Kessler changed them oftener.

I suppose one of the reasons I feel grouchy is that I want to get on with this war business and I feel we're just marking time. Well, I'm sure I'll have plenty of time to repent that feeling even though it may not be "repenting at leisure". feel this way because I miss you both very much.

June 9, 1943

I have just finished dressing for inspection and can't help but think that, if the Japs had ever landed here and the local washwomen had ever attacked them with any semblance of the ferocity with which they do our clothes, they would have met with an awful fate indeed! I honestly don't see how they could beat up a bunch of buttons so thoroughly, especially without beating, boiling or rinsing some of the soap out of the cloth at the same time. I honestly believe I could rinse one of my handkerchiefs in a bucket and have enough soap to bathe with!

I think that, after the war, I will finally accede to family demand and write a book. Undoubtedly the only suitable title would be "Gullible's Travels". We undoubtedly have covered as much ground as any unit in the US Army. My recollections of the last two or three years are filled with packing, loading, unloading and unpacking, making camp and breaking camp. However, the few really tranquil hours that I have had during that same period have been aboard ship or train with the roll checked and the doors locked. That is one situation where you can really control the troops with handiness!

The first man that I enlisted to be seriously injured was shot in the knee yesterday. I have never lost one of the men that I brought into the service and he is the first to have been painfully injured. His name is Newman Clark and he is just now 20 – a little fellow you probably won't remember. He is in Troop F now and was cleaning his pistol when it went off. I am afraid he will have a bad knee the rest of his life.

There is an unusual amount of bird life here, some varieties being very pretty; none, however, are what I would term exotic. We have found the "cow" birds that I described before, and there are lots of black and white birds similar to our pigeon except about half the size. There is a dove-type of bird, grayish-blue in color with an opalescent ruff that is very handsome. None of them make attractive noises, though, and most of the calls remind me of someone pulling a bucket of water out of a cistern without having oiled the pulley. (As a city girl, you may not appreciate exactly what I mean.)

Kessler is in a good humor these days for the first time since I have known him. He is like that famous bird that flew backwards all the time. Of course, all of us are a little keyed up and it is a real pleasure to see the outfit function.

I went into town this afternoon on an errand and found an English manual on model railways. It is really too simple for my purposes but thought I might keep it as a novelty. The first reminder of my hobby (if the little I did could be called a hobby) and I got quite a kick out of looking it over. If we ever get magazines any more, I'll subscribe to a model railroad magazine. But they seem to be out now so far as we are concerned. I really miss them, too.

Just like I miss you. I love you always.

June 11, 1943

You have no idea of how glad I am to have a little something set aside for you and Gayle in case of an emergency. I have always our insurance, and if anything should happen to me, you would get a final settlement of about $2,000 from the government and my $10,000 policy would give you small monthly payments. That isn't as much as I would like for you to have but, at that, is considerably better than nothing at all.

I am not trying to be morbid, although I am sure it sounds that way. I am your husband and responsible for you and Gayle. And, occasionally, it is necessary to face facts and figures, so don't think that I am just in a pessimistic mood.

I don't know whether you remember my 1940 reaction to the atabrine I took in Louisiana or not. Anyhow, it is really purgative for me. We started taking it last night at supper and I had to carry a roll of paper around in my pocket all night. It didn't seem funny to me at the time at all but it really was, I am sure, and I am going to laugh like hell when my sense of humor catches up with me.

Col. Miller continues as CO and I continue to marvel at how pleasant he is to work with. He is a fine man and I hope he can stay with us for the rest of our service. Col. Cunningham is still around, but has quite a bit besides us to worry about which is all to the good as far as we are all concerned.

Write to me often, baby, because I love you.

June 21, 1943

I was correct in my last letter when I said I probably wouldn't get a chance to write you for several days. I am now in New Guinea and have not had time to write since we arrived. I was in charge of our ship loading before we left and the unloading after we got here. It took 55 hours to unload 2 ships and I neither undressed nor slept during the entire period. I got a normal night's sleep Saturday night, though, and then loafed around Sunday, reading a little and putting a few refinements on my foxhole. My services as an "unloader" were requisitioned by higher command Sunday evening and I worked a crew from 8 until 6 this morning and have been reconnoitering for a good campsite today with Rupert. You can see that I am a little tired and excuse my poor

hand since I have already gone to bed and am under my
mosquito net.

New Guinea looks much like New Caledonia from a "sailor's-
eye" view, except that it is much more densely covered with
undergrowth, being entirely jungle. There are many more palm
trees here because we are much nearer the Equator than we
were there, and, also, because they are cultivated in huge
plantations all over the island. They are certainly the predominant
growth hereabouts and are very pretty since they are so graceful.

Apparently it rains here 20 hours a day average. My tent
leaks like a sieve after being loaded and unloaded so often and I
have my poncho spread over the top of my mosquito bar at the
moment. Everything is a muddy mess right now and bids fair to
remain so for some time. I have been told that the average
annual rainfall here is 300 inches, almost an inch per day, and I
can easily believe it.

I seldom become discouraged in the real sense of the word.
I have never really resented being here or having to submit to the
hardships that we meet. I only regret the things that I am missing
at home. (That may not make sense from that end of the line but
it is logical as hell from here.) If we could save time like we save
money, I wouldn't worry. I'd just put this period of our separation
in the bank to be used later on. But we can't do that and every
day I am away from you is a fraction of my life that is gone
beyond recall, and totally wasted. I often regret that the war
didn't catch me younger when I was single or that we had
married sooner and had more days of happy memories stored
up to bolster me. I intend to do my best and to get the job done
and come home. I love you both very much.

June 24, 1943

Jack, who is in 1st Squadron Headquarters again, and I started
on a walk this morning and wandered up into the hills, following
a little mountain stream. Suddenly we came upon a little pool
where a couple of native debutantes were bathing in water a

little less than knee deep. As they were not embarrassed, we tried not to be, and went on past to the edge of their village. It was, or appeared to be, a new village and was nice and clean. Most of the men were gone but we made friends with the kids and a few of the women before returning to camp. We ingratiated ourselves by giving them a few cigarets and then came back to camp.

After lunch, we went to another village where we took a bunch of pictures and bought some grass skirts and a few strings of beads made of some kind of native seed. We took pictures of the women, young and old, and have at least one sample of every type. Some of the old women (over 18 years) who have raised several kids, have breasts that resemble razor straps and look like they would have to throw them over their shoulders before they could run.

The grass skirts are made of palm fronds which are cut lengthwise in narrow strips about 2 feet long and ³⁄₁₆" in width and then woven into a heavier set of several strips which form the girdle. If I get a good one that is authentic and worth having (and hasn't been used), I will box it up and send it home.

The natives here are quite friendly and most of the boys are able to speak enough English to give directions. The older people do not speak so well, nor do the girls, who are kept pretty close to home and are somewhat shyer than the boys. It is hard to believe that people so seemingly gentle and naïve will bring you the head of a Jap for five dollars.

I know I told you of the IGD inspection we had while packing in New Caledonia. The colonel came over to see us today and brought us a copy of the report. An extract follows: "The following were found to be superior: combat efficiency, discipline and morale, the maintenance of arms, equipment and clothing, the quarters, kitchens and mess halls, the horses' picket lines and forage storage facilities, and so much of the horse equipment as was not packed." As a conclusion the following statement was made: "The general rating is superior."

Macho tribesmen from New Guinea making their presence felt.

You can judge by that how well the outfit maintained itself in the field and how well prepared we are to carry out any mission that may be assigned to us. Personally, I think we will make our own little dab of history in the near future. If so, I have no doubts as to the outcome. I am confident that we can handle whatever comes up and I have no fear that anything will happen to me, although a coconut fell out of a tree nearby this morning and nearly scared me to death. But don't worry. I intend to make it safely back home to you, because I love you.

June 29, 1943

I may have told you before that I have had my hair cut real close – not shaved, but about one inch long on top. It's a lot more convenient and much easier to keep clean. We do all our bathing in creeks or out of buckets. The creek is not over 6 inches deep so you can see that we have our sanitary problems. We have divided the beaches with the sharks and they get to use them unmolested for the first seven days in each week!

I am whiling away my spare time by teaching some of our detachment to send code by flashlight, a system used a great deal at sea to preserve radio silence. It is mildly interesting and helps me refresh my code, which I had almost lost – anything to break the monotony.

My biggest problem here is my ever-present hunger. I swiped a case of jungle rations and keep them in my tent to nibble on in my spare time. I just can't eat any more canned meat, fish or stew and hashes. Dehydrated potatoes are a crime so far as I am concerned. I do eat hot biscuits, butter and jam or jelly every meal, hot cakes and preserves every morning and canned fruit at nearly every meal, so don't worry. It's no worse here than New Caledonia.

We are truly starved for news since we see no magazines. If we ever get our back copies of *Life*, etc., it will be a regular riot for us, no fooling. Of course, we get a few bare facts about the rest of the world every day or so but no elaboration whatever.

Col. Miller has been sick but will be able to go on with us from here. He's a swell egg and I'd sure hate for him to get away from us. He's had the "flu" – one of the very few cases we have ever had. Most of us feel mighty good and darned few of the soldiers make sick call any more unless they get hurt in some way. We keep thinking Col. Cunningham will get promoted as he handles considerably more than just us these days. We hope he gets promoted to a better job and, especially, that he takes Hooper (Phearless Phil) with him.

I ran across a fellow named Pitman whose father, I think, used to know Dad years ago. I had a lovely meal as guest aboard his ship and he wants someone to write his folks about it. I sent his father's address to Dad and hope he will do it. Boy, did I go to town on fresh roast beef, mashed potatoes, gravy, etc. with hot tea and jello with fruit salad in it! Next war, I go Navy!

July 2, 1943 – V-mail
Our current mission was announced over the radio last night but I think I had better not give you any details. I will say that we are all well and in as little danger as I can imagine and still be doing our job. So there is nothing for you to worry about.

Life is more interesting now than it was a couple of months ago and the outfit is really functioning. I guess we feel more useful.

There are a thousand things I'd like to tell you, but I snatch the time for my letters from other things and they will have to wait. I can say 999 of them very simply, though, when I say, I love you.

July 6, 1943 – V-mail

I am sure our mail is not getting out, but I go ahead trying to write every day. I do not know why as there is so very little to say – maybe I am just trying to set you a good example.

We don't have any bathing arrangements yet and all of us smell like a bunch of goats, although I do try to sponge off daily. It is very hot here, especially when working in the jungle, and it rains at least 35% to 50% of the day and 100% of the night. I feel fairly well today as I have managed to stay dry most of the day for a change and we have our mess a little better organized. I'm not griping and we're getting along all right, so don't worry too much about us.

I had my picture taken with my platoon for a newsreel wearing coveralls and poncho with my overseas cap, dark glasses, and my carbine slung over my shoulder, so look for me at the movies from now on. I love you both very much.

July 7, 1943

It is awfully hot and still here in the jungle tonight, especially since I have had to close my tent all round in order to use my lantern to write this letter by. I just can't get any satisfaction out of writing V-mail to you for some reason. It seems somehow like a substitute and you know how I feel about substitutes!

It's a year now since I left you and I haven't accepted any substitutes yet. I'm weakening, though, and I may get off the path in another 25 or 30 years – that is just too long to hold out!

Seriously, if anyone ever had the opportunity to find out what he was missing, it is me. If you check my letters for the last year, I don't believe you can find a time where I have really seemed to regret missing shows, parties or the comforts of life. I just miss you and my baby and want to be with both of you so badly that it sometimes almost makes me cry. If I could spend 24 hours with the two of you, I'd be willing to be blindfolded and have cotton stuffed in my ears every time I got near to lights or music! I would even eat corned beef and like it and that is the ultimate in sacrifice so far as I am concerned.

Speaking of food, we subsist mainly on jungle rations that come in 12" square, waterproof boxes, each containing a day's food for four men. It contains a concentrated dry cereal for breakfast with dried milk, sugar and needing only the addition of water. There is a large can (about a quart) of powdered milk and one of Spanish peanuts, 4 small cans of beef and pork loaf fortified with vitamins, 4 boxes of pretty fair biscuits, a box of raisins, 8 packages of 10 cigarets, 4 packages of Life Savers or Charms, 8 cans of instant coffee (1 cup each), 4 small packages. of lemon powder, 4 packages of "instant" cocoa and 4 packages of toilet paper. They are the highest of quality and best packed food we have ever gotten but terribly monotonous. I am not being clever at all when I say that after eating them for a week, you think no more of eating than you do of using toilet paper. There is no such thing as mealtime. You just stick whatever you want to eat in your pocket in the morning and eat it as you go, as indifferently as you light a cigaret. Their chief virtue is that they are convenient and, I am sure, very nourishing. Also they contain no corned beef at all.

The Japs announced over their radio that they had cut off all our supplies and would starve us out. We don't get many laughs so someone listens to them every night and passes around the dope to all of us. If they just limit themselves to cutting our supply lines, we will be mighty fortunate people. We know it is not possible for them to cut off our food and, if they did, we could live off the country for a long, long time.

There are some hazards in war and all of us expect to meet them, but many troops are worse off than we are and we all appreciate our good fortune and go ahead with our job cheerfully. No one gets excited or jittery and upset except dear Hooper who everyone except the colonel knows is a damned fool anyhow. He still is playing soldier and hollers "wolf" at every turn. Without exception, every officer in the regiment would contribute a month's pay to get rid of him, preferably by violence.

We are in a situation here where rank alone is not enough. If you haven't got the stuff to go with it, you just get ignored. Several officers have told him off in the last few days, including Grant, and I think he is beginning to catch on and so is the colonel. Nothing ever bothers me and I just rock along from day to day, doing my work, and staying out of everyone's way.

There is a strong rumor here that all the troops who came over prior to October are to be returned home for Christmas. I don't put much stock in it, although I like to kid myself that it is true. If I am home for Christmas, we will have the biggest blowout you ever heard of. I'll have a dinner party for my family and yours, plus all our friends, at the fanciest joint in town. I'd even wear my service ribbons! That would really be something. Keep yourself young and happy. I love you.

July 8, 1943 – V-mail

I guess the power of suggestion just got to be too much for me. I've had a warm little glow in my heart all day just from the things I wrote you last night.

All of us hate the idea of having to go back to our old jobs after the war and we often discuss ways to get into something "good" when we get home. Jack and I have a new plan that figures out on paper as a real gold mine. We are going to pool our funds and open a Coca Cola plant in one of the larger Australian cities and teach the people bad habits. Of course, we'll have a new scheme by tomorrow but I still think that is the best idea we've had yet. Hope springs eternal. I love you.

July 11, 1943

For some reason, I got up this morning whistling classical tunes. Jack has started it also and we have about covered our limited repertoire. We started with "O, Patria Mia" and have run on through "Evening Star", "Liebestraum", the chorus from *Manon* and the "Berceuse" from *Jocelyn*. I just wonder if you ever use the Philco.

It has started the mid-morning torrent just now but I can just laugh at it (well, at the least, smile) today since I don't have to go out into it.

There is little, if anything, happening here that is hilariously funny. However, amusing things and funny situations do occur from time to time to lighten the depression. The first night we camped in the jungle the men chopped out little areas 15 to 20 yards apart. Now, there is an amazing amount of nightlife in the brush – snakes, birds, insects, lizards, etc. – and, after a night of rustling and crackling, punctuated by shrill cries from the crows, cockatoos, and parrots, the men have all moved gradually closer and closer to one another and are living in groups of a squad or more each. One of our boys went to the latrine in the night last night and missed his hammock on the way back. He shook another guy and said, "I'm lost. Where is my hammock?" The other must have been having a wild dream because he roused up and said, "Hell, I'm lost, too. Maybe we'd better stick together!" and went back to sleep.

Except where it has been cleared a bit for camps, you cannot see over 30 yards, at best, anywhere in the jungle. In our camp areas, where all the brush has been cleared, the taller trees furnish almost a perfect umbrella of foliage (it does leak, though) with the result that it is so gloomy that you can, at best, see maybe 100 yards. It is only on the cleared trails that you can have normal vision. I have lost my two best pairs of glasses, both dark and light, and have broken my lightweight reading glasses. That leaves me only my 2 GI pairs and I am really taking care of them.

When going through the jungle, the vines snatch at your arms and feet and you stumble over the tangled roots and rough outcroppings of coral. It is quite annoying. I caught my glasses on a limber vine yesterday and it jerked them off and literally flung them away. We looked for 30 minutes but couldn't find them.

Our legs, to the hips, are covered with bites and heat and chafed spots where our wet clothes rub against our skin. I have stood it all with at least a degree of equanimity – or, rather, I did until an ant stung me yesterday on what I used to consider my sexual organ! I must admit that got me!

I don't know whether you will recognize me when I get home. I have got pretty grey around the edges and, at the moment, I have what bids fair to be the longest, most English moustache in the Southwest Pacific! I'm sure it will be gone before I see you again, but I'll try to save you a picture of it.

Take care of yourself and of Gayle for me and be as happy as you can. I love you.

July 15, 1943

Singapore, Bali, Madang and Timor sound quite romantic. In fact, my experience is that everything connected with the South Seas sounds romantic but unfortunately, no matter how romantic it sounds, there has been nothing here for us but heat, insects, rain, mud, and other and innumerable discomforts, coupled with a tremendous amount of hard work. Just another case of proving the incompatibility of theory and practice, I suppose.

As you approach our island from the sea, it does give a lovely appearance. A beautiful beach of white sand spreads as far as you can see and is fringed with the inevitable line of coconut palms, the dark green of the jungle behind them serving

One of Lloyd's more unusual ways of saying
"I love you" to Virginia – the snail letter
dated July 15, 1943.

as a backdrop for the whole picture. The shore is so nearly level that little waves about a foot high cover the entire beach at high tide, making our occasional baths really delightful. The sandy bottom extends about 400 to 500 yards out into the bay and the water over it is a vivid green and is in contrast to the brilliant blue of the water beyond. It looks quite attractive to the arriving stranger. I can assure you that no one ever received a welcome of so much promise and met with so little fulfilment!

I just stepped outside to get a breath of air and found that there is a gorgeous moon just overhead and enough of its rays are sifting through the canopy of boughs to add a soft, somewhat luminescent glow to the jungle. It is as nearly attractive as I have ever seen it, although the moonlight makes me mighty lonesome for you. I love you.

July 20, 1943

I am glad my boxes got home in a hurry and before the boots had time to dry out or mold. I was really smart to send them as leather rots before your eyes here in this damp, hot climate. Also, I have no use for them whatever as I wear canvas, rubber-soled boots (called jungle boots) all the time. I hope you have received the New Guinea box with my lightweight shirts and the grass skirt. They may have thrown the skirt out en route, but I know it left New Guinea APO in the box.

I have been a little depressed all day as we started off the day in a miasma of heat that made me terribly nervous. It became considerably less sultry as the day progressed but I suppose I am not as flexible as I once was and I just went on being depressed. It is too easy to become depressed in these surroundings, especially since I have been away from you so very long and am so heartsick for you. I realize it and seldom allow myself to become actually morbid. Well, it just can't last forever. I wish they'd let the British and Russians do most of the fighting in Europe, though, and start a real push against the Japs.

I guess it is really better not to buy a house yet. If we stay in Fort Worth when I come home, I plan to go to Texas Christian University, to night school three nights a week. I have acquired a tremendous desire for knowledge since I came over here – not professional knowledge, such as law, but general information such as government, a language, literature or history. I think that we could really enjoy classes together if we picked subjects of mutual interest. For instance, I'd like to go back and study pure old grammar, especially sentence structure and punctuation.

I think probably the greatest thing that Mama ever did for me was to teach me to read. My earliest recollections are of her reading to me. By the time the war is over, I should be able to spend hours reading to Gayle. I'm sure she will be able to understand simple little stories by that time and I know I will enjoy it, too.

I get a good deal of pleasure out of planning our future and hers and enjoy talking to you about it. Take care of yourself and Gayle for me – and remember that I love you.

July 24, 1943 V-mail

The great day is finally here – the little folder of pictures has arrived! I can't begin to tell you how much they mean to me. They are lovely of both of you. The ones of you bring out all your good points without flattery.

I suppose you heard Knox's estimate of six more years of war – I may get to be a colonel yet! No matter how long the war lasts, I still believe I'll be home by Christmas, so there!

We heard tonight that Mussolini has resigned in favor of Marshal Badaglio who, as I remember it, is not pro-Nazi by any means. It doesn't necessarily signify that Italy will crumble, especially since there are so many German troops there, but it does prove that there is considerable dissatisfaction in Italy and that in itself will go a long way to destroy their combat efficiency. I predict that whole units of their troops will quit from time to time out of sympathy with us or because they have their belly full

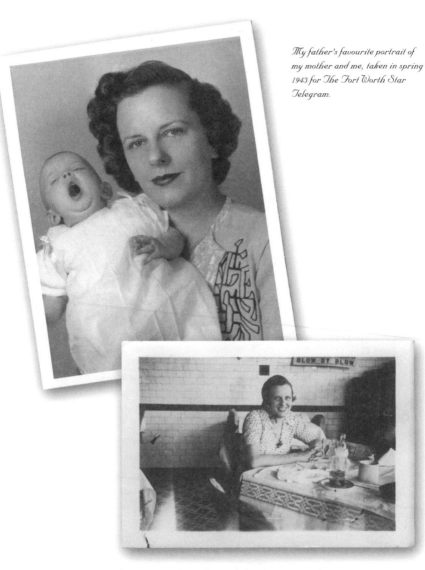

*My father's favourite portrait of
my mother and me, taken in spring
1943 for The Fort Worth Star
Telegram.*

*Virginia at the White House Café in Texarkana, where you
could get the best roast-beef sandwich in town for a quarter.
Lloyd always carried this snapshot in his wallet. It is still there.*

of a war not of their own choosing whether the government gives up or not. They are already so unreliable as to almost be a liability to Hitler. I certainly wouldn't feel safe with them protecting my flanks!

As you have gathered from the foregoing, I miss you badly and long to be with you every hour of every day – and twice that many of the nights. Take care of yourself and Gayle for me. I love you both.

July 30, 1943

I am sorry to have gone so long as three days without writing but have been busy unloading some of the supplies that the Japs were not going to allow to come through. I guess they must have gotten softhearted, as I can't see that we are apt to need anything for some time.

One of my men slipped his cable the other day and had to be put in the hospital under guard for observation. He was sent out of the area to Australia yesterday. He professed himself to be Jesus Christ and forced a bunch of men, at pistol point, to stay up several hours reading the Bible aloud to each other. We've had such things happen from time to time since leaving home and I suppose it is inevitable. It hasn't reached alarming proportions by any means, and I suppose there are an equal number in every group, regardless of circumstances. But he was so quiet and well behaved that it came as quite a surprise to me.

I am still getting a lot of pleasure from the photographs, although I have to keep them well wrapped on account of the moisture here. Getting them out for my almost daily inspection is a job of major proportions. But it's worth it. Looking at them is better for me than vitamins.

I have been able to get a box of Hershey's but feel sure that they will mold before I can eat them all. Everything molds or mildews here. If I looked in a mirror and found my tongue coated, I wouldn't be surprised – I'd just know it was mildew!

I still plan to be home by Christmas and hope Lady Luck will continue to be kind to us. I love you.

July 31, 1943

We have had several instances where officers have got themselves into trouble with their wives since we came over here, either because of something they did actually do or something someone said that they had done. As you know, these things usually irritate me a great deal. However, Capt. Hood, easily the most "innocent" person in the regiment, got himself into a jam recently that I cannot help but think is highly amusing.

The day I mailed you the last box (the one with the grass skirt in it), he was leaving the place where we had been as first part of a movement by sea to a new location. The post office was 10 miles away and accessible by small boat. He heard I had secured a boat and was going to mail you a package, and he asked me to mail a similar one for him, which I, of course, agreed to do.

As he was rather hurried, he just dumped odds and ends of superfluous junk into a ration box, and to fill it up, tossed in a bamboo drinking cup that some soldier had made for him and which contained a few bits of junk, pictures, etc. that he didn't have time to sort through. Much to his surprise, he got a hot letter from his wife who had found a box containing only one contraceptive – and, of course, she had drawn the only reasonable conclusion. She really raised hell.

Now, here's what makes it funny (or is it?): since we have been in the tropics, the soldiers have had little, if any, use for them although we have always maintained a supply to issue when they went on pass and wanted them at Fort Clark. We brought them with us and they were just in the way until someone realized that they were ideal for carrying matches, a watch, or any other small item that water could hurt. It is a common practice throughout the area, and I understand the Navy, at sea, have done it for years.

Well, there is no use going into further detail, as I am sure you can readily see what happened. It is really too bad, too, because Hood is as little of a ladies' man as you can imagine, and I have never even heard of him going to a dance since I have known him. But, I still think it's funny!

Anytime an officer makes any reasonably complicated plan for the future, he can be fairly sure that some phase of it will fall down on him. I read a joke that I thought reflected this attitude perfectly: a new paratroop officer was ready to make his first jump. His final instructions were, "Jump, count up to 10, then pull the first ripcord. If nothing happens, count another 10 and pull the second ripcord. There will be a jeep on the field to take you back home when you land." After following directions carefully, neither chute opened and he said, disgustedly as he fell to earth, "I'll bet the damned jeep isn't there either." Now that really is funny! At least to me.

I have been working at odd times on plans for a small model railroad layout for after the war. Had the day off today and finished it up. Drew scale plans accurate enough to use for building it when I get time. Having lots of time, I really made it complete – even figure percentages of slope to two decimals – and incorporated some very ingenious (for me) devices for getting lots of track into a little room without it being awkwardly arranged.

This is the last page of the last tablet that I have and I'll have to start using stationery, although I really don't like to. I like this ruled, lightweight paper much better. I am really lucky to have any at all and shouldn't complain. And it takes fully as long to "unstick" an envelope and a stamp as it does to write a letter.

I am still thinking of you every moment and living for the day that I can come home to you. In the meantime, I see you in every book I read, in every thought I have, and every dream. Wanting to come home to you and Gayle has become almost a mania with me, and I don't think I ever get the idea clear out of my mind, no matter what the circumstances. Write soon. I love you both.

August 3, 1943

I have just finished eating a great big green apple – the first fresh food we've had since early June – ambrosia was never better. We also got lemons, oranges, grapefruit, cabbage, potatoes and enough fresh meat for a meal or two. We really didn't get a great deal, but it couldn't have been more welcome.

We have the most anomalous weather conditions here, all completely unpredictable. The constant rains that we have had for over 36 hours had disappeared at daylight this morning, and instead, we have a soft, cool, bright morning with gentle breezes ruffling the treetops. It's the sort of morning that, in the early fall at home, makes you pull the covers up around your neck, stretch and go back to sleep, thankful that it is Sunday and you don't have to get up. There are other things you and I used to do on mornings like that, but I am sure I don't need to describe them.

At the moment, I am as awkward as a bear cub with boxing gloves on. I made a timely, but not too well directed, dive for my foxhole the other night and tore the skin on the backs of my knuckles a bit. It isn't of any consequence except that I can't get them to heal very fast because I keep forgetting and close my fist which breaks them open again.

My feet have healed beautifully, and I worked all day yesterday and most of last night without them bothering me a bit. I was careful not to get them wet this time, too.

Although I shouldn't brag, I still think that our luck has held pretty steady and I am relying on it to get us out and home by Christmas. Maybe a vain hope, but you have to have something to look forward to, you know. And that is what I have chosen, because I so want to come home. It must be because I love you.

August 7, 1943 – V-mail
We will soon be the proud proprietors of a really bombproof shelter where we can go back to sleep when we are interrupted during our night's rest. That will help, as it is a nuisance not to get enough sleep. We continue on our almost Sisyphean task of trying to tame the jungle – or at least that part of it in which we operate.

I am interrupted at every sentence as there is a crew felling trees and blasting stumps near us. I don't mind dodging Jap explosives but get a little tired of ducking our own after a while.

Will write again later. I love you.

August 9, 1943
I have just mailed you a V-mail dated August 10th. I don't know how I managed to get a day ahead of myself except that we have so little to remind us of the day or even the month. As a matter of fact, it is impossible, almost, to distinguish between the seasons out here except that one is wet and the other is wetter.

We had a real display last night with lightning and thunder enough to justify the literal flood of rain that followed it. Between occasional bombings, frequent blasting artillery target practice and thunder, I will either develop nerves of iron – or else be sent home as a victim of shell shock. (I am joking – nothing will happen to me to cause me to get sent home, well or otherwise!)

I had a very nice night, though, as it seems I was just disturbed enough to have a few dreams. I don't remember too much about them today, but if I hadn't been dreaming about you, you'd be justified in divorcing me for infidelity.

As I have often told you, sex seldom crosses my mind any more, and it is only in these occasional dreams that I come to realize how much I want you that way, too. My conscious desires are centered more upon the constant need that I have of your companionship and the comfort of your presence in our own home. Still, it's nice to be reminded from time to time so pleasantly of the physical pleasure that we have shared and to know that we have more to look forward to in the early (I hope) future.

There's no way for anyone to know what will happen to us when we leave here. Too much depends upon the way the war goes, and I don't believe MacArthur himself could do more than guess at our future. That is, if he knows where we are!

Being here seems such a waste of my life to me. I never counted myself as living until I married you, so 27 years was thrown away to start with. Now I am losing years of my real life with you, and they can never be regained, ever. Of course, we can spend lots of time trying to make up for them when we are together again!

Take care of yourself and Gayle for me, and remember that I love you.

August 14, 1943

You mention your pleasure in recollections of our life together, and I often feel the same way. You can't force yourself to remember and enjoy, though. It just has to creep up on you at odd moments. "The most tender and valuable memories of man are those which elude him time and again, playing tag down the glades of the past, and permitting him only the briefest glimpse of their beauty as they vanish before him."

I read a thought the other day that expressed something that has often occurred to me. That is, that we really know little about the other people with whom we are associated, even those with whom we are on a truly intimate basis. Certainly most of what we know of anyone is just what that person is willing to trust us with.

There really isn't a great deal to write about over here. I could say, as I used to do, that it is beastly hot today (it is), and that my lunch of corned beef was not fit to eat (it wasn't), but I get as tired of griping as you probably do of hearing it in my letter. So this, in a way, is one of my antidotes for it.

I have two new possessions that I haven't had a chance to tell you about. One is GI hunting knife with heavy blade and scabbard. The other is a cat that has adopted me. The Chaplain brought a box of cats with him from our last station and this one seems to have strayed from his fold and has just flatly moved into my tent, often jumping into my lap and curling up for an hour or two while I am reading.

I promised to stop this early this afternoon, and it's getting dark now so I guess I really will stop. I got a ride to the Chaplain's tent and found some books to read. Thomas Hardy's *Under the Greenwood Tree* and Conrad's *Nostromo*. I also sneaked in a couple of two-bit detective stories.

I think of you and Gayle and home continuously and long for the day when we can be reunited again. Write me soon and often and remember constantly that I love you.

August 23, 1943

Your letter of July 7th was very dear to me as it was written at a time when you thought I was going into actual combat (and I had just barely found out we were not). We were very fortunate to find conditions favorable and expected that we might have to fight our way ashore or be prepared to resist an attack at any time after landing.

Well, it is no secret now that none of this happened, and of course, we were all considerably relieved although I think we were ready for whatever was coming and not a man would have turned back.

Bombing is primarily a nuisance unless they happen to destroy material, and anyone with good sense can protect themselves to a great extent. I have had a string of ten bombs land in front of me, the nearest within less than 100 yards and the furthest less than 500 yards away and was perfectly safe. If you get away from potential targets and into a slit trench or dugout, any good insurance company would issue you a policy on the spot! So there is no more danger here than there was when I was breaking horses – and really less, in my opinion. It is a little hard on the nerves momentarily but I find you get over that quickly.

I had better quit now and try to sneak a little nap (you shouldn't keep me awake so much at night). Don't worry about me at all. I certainly don't worry any more. If you worried at all here, you'd have to worry all the time, so I just quit worrying at all. I love you.

September 4, 1943

I really hadn't planned to write to you tonight but, somehow, it is always a little hard to go to bed without it. Sort of seems like the day is incomplete, or something.

I think that when this is over, my bitterest recollections will not be a hate of the Germans or the Japs, nor even of a certain colonel. Instead, I am sure it will be of the sheer, almost unbearable, boredom with which we are constantly faced. It nearly runs you crazy at times with no magazines, no books, and no new associates. I've read the few books that we have in the regiment that are of any consequence, once or twice each, and have read many of the dull, uninteresting tomes that make up the bulk of our "library". Most of them were donated by an appreciative public whose most patriotic gesture, probably, to date has consisted of selecting carefully the cherished books from their shelves that they enjoyed least, if they had ever read them at all.

I get so goddamned tired of reading articles and ads in the magazines that we get from two to five months after publication, about the fine food, deliciously prepared and scientifically balanced as to nutritive and vitamin content, and of the wonderful books, the correspondence courses, the unit radios and victrolas, the song albums and entertainers that our dear boys get in the overseas theaters.

Well, I've been over here nearly 14 months and so far I've seen Joe E. Brown last Spring and a second rate magician whose only real asset was the fact that he at least had been willing to come out and do his best.

We have about a half dozen films on the island all of which have been shown a minimum of three times apiece and to which we all go religiously every time they are shown. It wouldn't be so bad if you thought you had half a chance of going nuts but it's really hell to know that you're going to have to stay sane and just endure it on and on, ad infinitum, ad nauseam!

We are here, we came willingly, and we'll still be doing our best when it's all finished but some of the baloney is just a little hard to take. We certainly can understand the difficulties of supply that causes our food to be monotonous and unpalatable and our mail to be often late and packages to be uncertain but we get tired of reading the hooey written by some guy who doesn't know what he's talking about telling how wonderfully we're being taken care of. The Navy's fresh meat and the Marines' beer ration doesn't help any either. I don't know how they get the breaks but they sure do.

We had a band concert today and all of us enjoyed it. They play the same old moth-eaten tunes and never seem to get any new music. It creates a little diversion and they really put out in their effort to be entertaining.

We're a sorry-looking bunch with nearly everyone as thin as a rail and some looking downright emaciated. Everyone is yellow or light green from constant absorption of atabrine. Actually, we are all reasonably healthy, I think, and we certainly have been able to combat malaria with a high degree of efficiency. We've had two cases out of our squadron in all the time we have been exposed. That's quite a record for a place that is notoriously ridden with the stuff. Our resistance is bound to fall as time goes on, though, and some of the men tend to get careless, too, about the elaborate precautions we try to observe.

Tommie Driggers just came over for me to censor one of his letters. He's so shy that he just can't stand to have someone read his mail and he knows I skip the passages that are obviously personal. Censoring mail isn't one of my duties at all and I certainly refuse it for everyone else, although I have censored Frank Hook's and Tommie's all the time we've been gone. I just can't stand to read other people's mail for some reason.

We have a new rumor that sounds good although we have little (none at all, in fact) confidence in it. Someone said General Johnson made a speech in which he said that he was glad to announce that his brigade would be reunited on the border before Christmas, and definitely stated (supposedly) that we'd be home. He probably said it alright as it sounds just like him – but we'd almost have to be packing now to make it – and we certainly are not packing. In fact, we are becoming so thoroughly dug in over here that I expect to sprout roots almost any day!

Rupert is just about due for another health failure and, if he has one, that will help give me something to occupy my mind. I am still surveying officer, summary court, etc., and have also been made claims officer for the task force. Guess I'll end up counting coconut stumps to find out how much we owe the local plantation owners for coming up here to protect them.

Write as often as you can and take care of yourself for me. We've got to make up lots of lost happiness when I get back to you. I love you.

September 8, 1943

I was a better prophet than I thought when I told you last night that Rupert was due for a spell in hospital. He must have been reading over my shoulder, as he packed up and went over there this morning. He has pains but no one seems able to tell much about them. Well, it "semi-solves" my problem of being perpetually bored, anyhow, as running the squadron will keep me busier.

I am certainly glad that my daughter can look up at the full moon and enjoy it. Unfortunately, I don't suppose I'll ever see a full moon again without subconsciously thinking, "Well, will we get it again tonight?" We've certainly had little cause for complaint here of late on that score, though, and even the "nervous" boys are relaxed. We still observe adequate precautions, though, and will continue to do so. I can guarantee that if the first raid doesn't get you, any later ones will have little chance. You don't have to hear them whooshing down many times before you dig yourself a nice, deep hole – and use it, too! The chance of being bothered is pretty negligible really. That doesn't keep you from being nervous while you hear the planes buzzing around overhead, though.

Actually, the greatest danger to personnel is when a bomb hits a tree and explodes in the air. The answer to that is to have your hole covered over with logs and sandbagged on top of that. The least I can say for our shelter is that it is more than adequate! So, since it would take a direct hit and we're not camped close to any of the likelier targets, we are really pretty safe.

Every man that I brought into the service three years ago is alive today and that is a grand feeling for me when I realize it. I have always sort of felt that I held them in "trust" for their families at home, most of whom I knew, and I hope some day to personally deliver every one of them to their homes again.

I am sure you realize that it would take a miracle to get me home for Christmas. I really don't think we'll have to stay out here until the end of the war, though. I think that by the time Hitler is licked, and fresh troops are available to relieve us, we'll be replaced. Certainly, by that time we'll have to be pulled back to a temperate climate for extended recuperation.

By the way the Russians are going these days, Germany's doom is quickly being sealed and, if they keep on this way, the European war could easily be over by early next year. Our greatest hope is for Mountbatten to get on to India and start hitting Burma. We feel that is where our salvation lies (or is that "lays"?).

It is pretty lonesome around here at night. We have our three tents all facing on a semi-circular clearing back in the jungle a ways and none of the others live here at the moment. Jack is on outpost, Jeffress is on detached service to another outfit, and Rupe is in the hospital. I'm becoming such a recluse, though, that I don't really mind. I have a little spare time world of my own and I almost actively resent anyone intruding upon it. It really isn't good for me, I guess.

I have enjoyed the mail tonight and will try to be more cheerful from now on. Maybe we'll be together sooner than we think. I love you.

September 10, 1943

I am attaching this little ring for Gayle. I beat it out of an Australian sixpence so at least it is made of good material (silver). I've never been able to give her anything that I've made myself and little enough that I've had made for her by others, so I hope she can keep this. It's a little large for a seven-month-old gal but she will grow up to it too soon, I'm afraid.

We had a pretty good day yesterday and today. Italy surrendered, fresh meat for lunch, seven letters night before last, another from Mama today, a USO show featuring a Met singer named Hatfield, accompanied by an excellent piano accordionist yesterday afternoon, and a brand new double feature at the movies last night, also a bunch of magazines.

Be careful of the both of you and maybe we'll be together sooner than we can believe. I love you.

September 16, 1943

I undoubtedly had the unhappiest dream I've ever had in my whole life early this morning. It seems utterly silly by the light of day with me awake, but I really went through the agony of hell while it lasted. I dreamed that I came home and found you were living with some other guy and had been supporting him from your allowance and that both of you claimed Gayle. Can you imagine such a silly business? I was really shaken when I woke up.

Actually, the whole thing is easily explained as it followed the general outlines of a sorry book about a sorry woman that I've been reading the last day or so. It's sort of funny now, of course, but it certainly wasn't at the time.

It's now after supper and I am all set for a long evening of monotony. Especially will it be monotonous if we have an alert, as it gets awfully tiresome just sitting in a shelter waiting for something to happen. We talk some, of course, but have long since worn out the customary topics of conversation. We're even tired of talking about coming home – and that was the most durable subject we've ever had!

I haven't lost interest in thinking about coming home, though, and it is my primary "extra-curricular" activity. We heard on the radio that Lae has fallen as of today and that is extremely good news. Progress out here has been greatly accelerated during the past two months and every minor victory hastens "the day".

The people at home shouldn't relax now and get the idea that the war is practically in the bag, though. Most of the gains out here are what we refer to as local victories and, although each is important in its own right, no one of them alone is of any strategic importance. The great thing, of course, is that in the aggregate they do spell a step toward the end of the war.

Kessler has been wanting a little change, and I've put him to operating the switchboard from four in the afternoon until 10 at night. He seems to enjoy the responsibility and still has plenty of time to take care of my stuff. He misses all the shows, of course, but they are usually so bad that it doesn't make any difference. He has been more cheerful lately than ever before. He was over here griping the day Rupert went to the hospital and I urged him to transfer back to his friends in Troop C. He agreed at first and then backed out. He knows damned well that he'd have to stand guard duty, KP, etc. up there, none of which our detachment has to do here.

My greatest desire for food is for good soups, salads, cottage cheese, cold drinks and cold desserts. I guess that this is because we never have any of these things out here. We'll certainly have to get a new and larger icebox when I get home.

Write me as often as you feel able and don't work yourself too hard. I want you to be well and happy when I come home. I love you.

September 22, 1943

Mama is going to mail some homemade candy and cookies and, of course, they'll be ruined before they could conceivably get here. There's nothing to do about it, I guess, as I don't want to hurt her feelings. Anything that isn't securely sealed hasn't got the chance of a snowball in hell of ever arriving here fit to eat. There's not much of anything I want anymore – I just want to come home.

The war news continues to be good. I rather doubt the authenticity of the purported coup that they claim the 100 German generals are planning for the elimination of Hitler. I don't doubt but that they see the handwriting but feel it is a little early to expect a crack in their political setup as yet. I think Japan is stronger today than they were a year ago and will continue so until we get into position to pound the hell out of their production areas. That has been primarily what has taken the starch out of German forces.

I really loved both of your letters and I sincerely believe that the big half of our separation is past. Less than another year should see us reunited and it will surely be forever this time. I actually can't remember our being separated for over a few hours before I left home unless it was thrust upon us by circumstances, and I know we'll cling together more strongly than ever when I finally come home. I have never loved you more than I do at this moment, and I know that that love will last forever and never waver.

September 23, 1943

I must admit that I got a tremendous feeling of love and tenderness from what you said about our physical separation and of your plan for us to have a second honeymoon before we bet back home to family and friends. I've felt the same way for so very long that it was good to have you say what you thought about it. Of course, I know how you feel about these things, and I know you miss me as much as I miss you. Nevertheless, I was never more in the mood to hear you put it into words.

Every day I become more and more convinced that the
generals are completely out of psychological touch with the
officers and the men in the field. If they could understand that
the bulk of their personnel have no stake in the Army itself and
are only here to protect their country, they would certainly
change their approach. So long as we don't lay ourselves open
to court-martial action, they just can't scare us by their tongue
lashings nor with the threat of demotion, reclassification or even
discharge for we are all in the enviable position of having little to
lose under any circumstances. They just can't see that we'd
respond 100% better to a fairer attitude and a system of
judicious praise and reward for work well done. We have had a
very pleasant morning but it has now settled down to a long,
drawn-out rain – almost a deluge at the moment. What you'd
call a general rain over there. I have too much respect for you to
tell you what we call it over here!

As luck would have it, Col. Miller called just after I got back.
He's a good guy. A little unimaginative, a good bit of an old
maid, but a thorough well-educated, intelligent gentleman if I
ever saw one. And as fair, according to his own ideas, as it is
humanly possible to be. We are glad to have him acting as
regimental commander not only because we like and respect
him so well, but because it also means a minimum of
Cunningham, Phearless Phil, et al.

This is really as dark and gloomy a day as you can imagine
but I am not even remotely depressed by it, which is unusual. I
guess it's from the pleasure I got from your letters and which is
still lingering in my heart. Write soon and take care of yourself
and Gayle for me. I love you.

September 25, 1943

You mention our staying in the service. As I see it, that is a
problematical proposition right now. I'm afraid it will mean
extended Foreign Service after the war, and I feel sure you'd be
opposed to that. You and Gayle could probably join me in a

year, but a year is a long time to me. It would offer considerably more security for us than anything else, but Col. C. has ruined a lot of my appetite for the Army. You might not always be serving under such a thoroughgoing heel, though. This seems to be just another question for time to settle. I'd like to hear your views.

Everything has been uncertainty for me for so long now that I have become almost accustomed to it. I can no more imagine where I'll be six months from now than I can imagine myself as Queen of England. So any planning I do now is largely for the entertainment value in it.

Rupert came over tonight for about an hour. We live about 25 feet apart and don't visit much as we can holler anything we've got to say to each other. I ought to be glad of the company, I guess, but really am becoming such a recluse that I almost resent the intrusion – especially if it is the chaplain who is undoubtedly the shallowest and most annoying clerical figure I have ever know. Brother Mac of Brackett would look like the Archbishop of Canterbury up side this punk – and he wasn't much either.

I gave up and went to bed last night and it is now Sunday morning. A bunch of trucks kept buzzing back and forth so I didn't get much sleep. I am a bit nervous and sleepy this morning especially as it is really a sticky, oven-hot day. Kessler has been slack about my laundry, too, so I'm having to wear denims which are heavy, hot and uncomfortable. Life is so constantly uninspiring here that I hate to get after him.

Rupert and I now have a shower bath. We got an oil drum and raised it on poles, borrowed a showerhead from a ship and do very well. We spread an old tarp over it to catch rainwater and it stays full all the time. Not bad!

We've had it pretty quiet lately and are all duly appreciative. It sure gripes us to sit down in a hole and get bombed at without having any personal recourse, even though you know you're at least as safe as you'd be driving a car at home.

Write as often as you can, sweetheart, because your letters are my greatest pleasure, for sure. And take care of yourself and Gayle for me. I love you.

September 30, 1943

I'll admit that at this moment, I'm lower than a whale's belly in all categories – mentally, physically, morally (ha ha) and spiritually. Financially, too, as we all just kicked in $26 apiece on an officers' club. It's a hell of a note when an officers' club, located on a deserted island and built with GI materials, costs more than it cost to belong to a good one at home where there were weekly dances, a swimming pool, golf and polo. And all I hear about this one is that there will be a bar.

Dad tells me his business is mighty good and I'm glad to hear it as he certainly is due a break. I'm afraid it's pretty tiring on him, though, as I am sure help is scarce. He also told me about taking Gayle out to feed the ducks and I can't tell who got the most fun out of it between the two of them.

Life goes on in the same old way here day after day. Just our regular routine with nothing to break the monotony except some of the most cleverly constructed rumors you can imagine. When Dante tried to picture hell, he put a sign on the door reading, "All ye who enter here, abandon hope." So, while there is life there is hope to keep you out of hell. I love you.

October 3, 1943 – morning

Rumors are still rampant here that we're to be sent home next spring. As a charter member of the Skeptics' Society, I have my doubts about it, though.

I have mentioned my fear for the future before. I haven't tried to stress it because I have had enough confidence in your common sense and understanding not to think it was necessary. I may be a bit morbid because of the circumstances in which I live – but I don't think I am exaggerating the probabilities to any great extent.

I have no particular fear of being killed in combat. My greatest fear has always been of coming home crippled and being a burden to you and Gayle. It has hurt me a lot in the past not to be able to give you things you needed. I don't want that sort of thing ever to happen again. And you can be sure that I won't come home in that condition as it would be too simple to rectify en route.

I have no doubt that there are plenty of draft-dodging bastards around making a good living for the first time in their lives off of our necessity for supplies, and who are plenty willing to lay up with the temporary war widows, sympathizing with their unhappy lives and feeding their egos. But I am just as sure that when the women become eligible for marriage by virtue of actually becoming a widow and really need something fed besides their poor, lonely egos, that those men will suddenly become very elusive, indeed.

Now, we are convinced that we are going to see action in the not too distant future. The only thing we don't feel certain of is where and when, although we have some pretty definite ideas on that, too. I think I'll live through it and come home reasonably sound. But it's time I quit gilding the lily and told you just how things are so you can take stock of yourself and resources in an intelligent manner and prepare yourself reasonably for any eventuality.

But rest assured that I'll be home in one piece and as soon as I can if I have any say in the matter. I love you both.

October 3, 1943 – evening

We have all kinds of things happen to us out here. I have ringworm on the inside of my right thigh. I have a topical fungus growth over the ball of my left foot (not athlete's foot) and an infected bite on the back of my left ankle that has made a superlative sore about half an inch wide by two inches long. I also have a heat rash around my waist under my belt that seems almost permanent. None of it is really serious, I'm sure, but it is hell not to be able to sleep at night because you want to scratch so damned badly. Some of the soldiers, who lack the self-discipline to keep from scratching, have sores all over their legs and there's quite a bit of vine poisoning of a sort similar to poison ivy. The worst thing yet, though, has been a few cases of filariasis, a disease transmitted by mosquitoes that results in a tremendous swelling of the testicles and is only curable, so far as I can find out, by castration!

It doesn't make you any more cheerful, either, when you hear some soldier's story of his wife getting pregnant a year after he has left home or who has spent her allotment and all the money he has been able to save and which he has foolishly trusted to her. These things are the result of hasty and ill-considered marriages and you seldom hear of it happening to a couple who have been married over a period of years and for whom fidelity has become a habit instead of just an ideal.

The great mistake that separated couples make is in thinking they can have a little fun and not shoot the works. I really think that most people have the best intentions in the world. But they feel they can go out with a friend of the family safely, then one thing leads to another and away they go! It just isn't possible for anyone accustomed to complete sexual satisfaction to stop at half measures once they start, and I don't believe there are any exceptions except those who just refrain from temptation completely. It seems that humanity's great frailty is that it is so human! (That is Hunnicutt's profundity for today.)

Thinking about this just makes me miss you more. Write to me soon, sweetheart, because I love you.

October 8, 1943

Here I am, ensconced in the comparatively lovely luxury of my new hut. As I told you in the V-mail I wrote this morning, it isn't nearly as nice as the one I had before I came here – but it does keep the mosquitoes out and I do have the most unusual pleasure of an electric light!

I guess it is just my perverted and somewhat macabre sense of humor, but I can't help but laugh at the little pre-bedtime arrangements I make every night and the contrast with the way it used to be at home with you – just locked the doors, put a screen in front of the fireplace and went to bed. Here I come in, take off my shirt, put a fresh packet of cigarets and matches in it, lay out my house slippers (a pair of "cut down" GI shoes) where I can get into them easily, and put my shirt and pants where I can find them without showing a light.

The reason is obvious, I'm sure. The odds are at least fair that I'll hit my little shelter before morning – and once I get in there, I sure don't like to have to come out for anything I have overlooked taking the first time. We get ample warning in every instance and I really think I'd be safe enough in my tent. I'll probably always think so too as I certainly don't intent to stay there and test it out! Fortunately, most of our alerts don't materialize into anything of consequence to us. But we play it plenty safe so far as it is possible and take cover at even a suspicion of Jap planes. I want – and intend – to live a long time – and, if I don't it won't be for being too lazy to get off my fanny and get under cover!

Rupert and I are bumming our electricity from some of our naval friends. We put in the wire ourselves and it is really a convenience. And it is bound to be better for my eyes although it is a little hard to get accustomed to. My lantern is an unusually good one but the globe tended to distort the light into alternate light and shadowy lines and I had to be careful that the most "select" streak was on what I was drawing or reading. I only have a 50-watt bulb but it is pretty bright and clear. If these conveniences continue, I'll soon be trying to flush the latrine.

I've lost quite a little sleep the past two nights, so I'll close for now. I love you and miss you constantly and hope that our separation cannot last more than a few months more. I feel I've about had my share. Write soon. I love you.

October 10, 1943

I am writing this a special "flash" news item. I know you will be happy with us to find that the colonel has finally been promoted to brigadier general. We had all about given up hope and consider that we're mighty lucky – I am sure you know why! Now Col. Miller can be promoted and become regimental commander.

When word came about the colonel's promotion, Rupert wanted to call him up and congratulate him but I razzed him out of it. He has torn off in his jeep now, and I am sure he's headed for an early seat on the bandwagon. Boy, if he's not a double-dyed hypocrite, then I never saw one! He's called that old man everything in the book behind his back and kissed his fanny to his face ever since I can remember. That would take something of a contortionist, I know, but when it comes to combining backbiting with fanny kissing, Rupert is undoubtedly tops. He also talks bigger about what he is going to do – and does less – than anyone I ever saw. He reminds me of one of those tarzanesque birds that beats on its chest and then goes into a coma!

I hope you got the snapshots of Gayle that you mentioned. I am anxious to see just how she looks these days. I know she is getting cuter and brighter every day and is a lot of pleasure to you in every way. Be sure and shove them right on through.

I may be doing the wrong thing but I intend to go see Miller and tell him I expect to be counted in definitely on any promotions he has under consideration. I can't see how I could lose by it, really. Anyhow, sitting back and keeping my mouth shut certainly hasn't done me any good. Of course, the odds are against me since Clyde will become executive and that puts McMains in line for 2nd Squadron – and justifiably so, I might add. It would make me pretty sore if they promoted Rupert and I didn't get this outfit. I'm still going to try, though. And I am not going to do any consulting among my friends. Every time anything happens around here, each guy goes to figuring what he can get out of it – and I don't see any use in continuing to be a chump.

Dearest Virginia

Well, I know I can't send any more pages on one stamp so will close. I love you.

October 12, 1943 V-mail

We have been bombed again and guess you know about it as it was announced on the radio the day following. It was the largest to date but when you realize how carelessly they seem to fling those things about, it tends to make you a bit nervous for an hour or so. Well, it's all a chance proposition just like nearly everything else you run across in life. You just take what precautions you can and hope everything will be alright.

I'm getting to be a pretty good "hoper" – but, hell, I get plenty of practice. I keep hoping for mail, for cool weather, for dry weather, for decent food and a chance to come home and dirty up your sheets. If that ain't overworking my "hoping department", I don't know what you could call it.

I still haven't gotten any mail so have definitely decided to cut you down to one letter a day. And, if the situation continues without improvement, I may take one day off a week without writing you at all. Now, let that be a lesson to you!

Rumors still fly thick and fast – and there still are few facts to back them up. I do feel like the big raid on Rabaul that was announced yesterday was the beginning of the end for this immediate vicinity and that things will be a little safer for us for a while.

We have it all doped out that we will go to one of about 14 different places when we leave here – and I have no reason to give any one destination precedence over another. Just hope that if we don't come home for a while, we don't go back to any place we've already been. I'll take something new, myself.

They just turned out my lights (it's 10 p.m.) and I doubt if Kessler has any gas in my lantern, so I'll have to close. I miss you every moment of the day – and immeasurably at night. I guess we just don't know our capacity for loneliness and unhappiness until we have to endure it. I love you.

October 15, 1943 – V-mail

The cattle business seems to have improved a great deal. I'm sure Dad is pretty busy and I hope it will continue long enough for them to get caught up financially. If they ever get the house paid for, I'd feel better about it as they are getting pretty old and tired and it would be a refuge. It must be hell to live all your life and still have but little when it is over. Of course, my folks and your grandparents have put everything into their kids and that must be some satisfaction, especially since none of us are in the penitentlary at the moment!

Kessler has just come over to measure my hut for an awning. A driving rain blows in at the front pretty badly although the sides and back stay dry enough. I'll have to quit in a minute to help him, I guess. I love you.

October 17, 1943

Got your letter last night about 10 p.m. and was certainly glad to get a little shower in the middle of the mail drought we have been having. We have reason to think there will be some mail today in quantity. Sometimes we get fooled on this – but sometimes we are right, so we can always hope a little.

Now you can just turn the next paragraph over to your complaint department. Your letter #145 dated October 3rd was mailed 13 days after your letter #143 and the missing #144 was the only letter you wrote between them, making an average of one letter every 6½ days. The two I have are V-mails, which have all the advantages of post cards with no pretty pictures! Young lady, that just flat isn't enough mail for me, so you can do one of two things – either write longer letters by air mail or else write shorter ones more often.

In fact, if I was teaching you a course in correspondence, you'd have to work pretty hard the rest of this semester to keep from flunking the course! Your letters, with one or two exceptions, have always been rather short. I can understand that as there is really so little of consequence to write about after 15 months. Lately, however, they have gotten further and further apart and you've fallen back on V-mail more and more. Some of them have sounded almost perfunctory.

I'm really not seriously complaining but am kidding to a great extent. God knows it is hard to keep letter writing from being a chore under the circumstances. Of course, I write you longer letters and more often because it is my chief diversion after I finish my work. But I don't have a house and a baby to take care of, relatives to visit, or picture shows to go to occasionally. You do have more to occupy your time than I do and the last thing I would intend to imply is that you should neglect any of them. In fact, I count on things like that greatly to keep you young and happy for me and to compensate you for some of the unhappiness that necessarily goes with our present separation. Since I am so sure that you will not seek any of the diversions that would forever hurt our present or future happiness together, I'd sure be selfish to ask you to deny yourself any of the few little pastimes that are open to you. But don't leave your old man over here holding the (mail) bag – and it empty – too much!

Col. Miller has his papers in for his promotion to full colonel. He has indicated that he plans for the regiment to remain in "status quo" until he finds out who will be transferred to the island command. My attitude is that, if I get something out of it, then it's fine; if I don't, to hell with it! However, it would be foolish for me to say that I don't want promotion or that I won't do all I can to get it.

I still do a little court-martial work in my capacity as Summary Court. I am not a member of any higher courts right now and am glad of the change. I really enjoyed my outside work in the court at Noumea, but, frankly, our own regimental courts are so ineptly operated by all concerned that I'd rather not be fiddling with them.

Hell, I'm out of paper – will go inspect the troop area and write more later. I love you.

October 18, 1943

I got your letter #144, dated 9/28, last night, and I am naturally furious about it because it made such a thorough heel out of me over the letter of complaint I sent you yesterday morning. It was definitely unkind of you to send me such a nice, sweet, newsy letter – and long, too – just when I had gone to so much trouble to make you feel bad. An unfair advantage, I calls it.

I have been nervous and upset lately and have had a terrible time getting to sleep at night. After I got your lovely letter, I went to bed and slept like a baby. I can't tell you how much that sort of letter means to us out here. A person who hasn't actually lived here just couldn't know, no matter how sympathetic their nature.

There are a number of reasons for my mental unrest. Fortunately, you are still all right as long as you can realize just what is bothering you and take the necessary action to combat it. The siege of rumors we have undergone of late has been a very disturbing factor. Some of them have been of Machiavellian cleverness in their construction and difficult to disprove, although I think we have finally punctured every one. The hell of it is that you are so damned anxious to believe you are going home soon that you can't help but get a lift out of them even if they are so fantastic as to be utterly false.

We were sitting at the table the other night talking about rumors and I told the boys that we'd just start a rumor manufacturing contest and see who could make up the most fantastic one, hoping to ridicule rumors to such an extent that we could just make jokes out of them in the future. I started off by telling them that I had heard that the bulk of the combat troops here were going to India as soon as the next phases of local actions were over and the few troops who had been here the longest would be sent home. I further told them that, rather than guard two convoys, we'd all go to India in one huge convoy and that those going home would continue on from there to New York. Hell, by daylight it was all over the squadron! And I had made it up right in front of them, and they had added details to it from their own minds as I went along and knew positively that the whole story was the sheerest of fabrications. Just goes to show what flimsy straws the human mind will grasp in its effort to keep hope alive. Boy, this would be a psychiatrist's heaven out here! Of course, getting to come home and making a trip around the world at the same time does sound pretty good. I wonder if it could be true?

I never loved you more and I did think your letter the best I've ever had. I love you.

October 25, 1943

I'll be glad to get some of our Christmas cards and I am sure your method of having our names printed on them is absolutely correct. I doubt that there are 25 people that I can think up from here – but I did last year and suppose I can again. I'll enjoy trying. There's one nice thing about making a Christmas card list: it forces you to sort of recapitulate your stock of friends (inventory is a better word) and, of course, as you add each name you are reminded of some of the pleasant things that cause that person to be your friend.

I read in a magazine that the belief of most people in the US that a hole dug straight down would come out in China was incorrect. It said instead that a hole dug "vertically" down from Dallas would come out in the Southwest Pacific area. That's just the way I've felt for a long time! That I am just as far from home as it is possible to get. I must be psychic. And it is sure hell to be on the opposite side of the world from you and our gorgeous baby. Your letters bridge the gap a bit – but the gap is so very wide that, as good as your letters are, it is a pretty slender bridge. Like the strand of a spider's web, though, it is the strength of the tie that matters and I know that our attachment to one another will never be severed no matter what the circumstances may be. G. K. Chesterton once said, "The way to love anything is to realize that it might be lost." Nothing was ever truer! And although I feel reasonably sure that nothing can happen to me here or to you there to destroy our future happiness, I cannot help but be tortured at times by the realization that something just barely could happen to keep us apart. And that torture is a pleasure in a way because it makes me realize more fully that I love you.

October 30, 1943 – V-mail

Another day has passed and no mail. If this keeps up, you soon won't have any male either – or, at least not this one. If I don't hear from some of you pretty soon, I am going to go into a decline like a mid-Victorian lady and just wither away. It hasn't been quite so bad the last few days, though, as no one else has been getting any mail. It isn't "misery loves company" attitude, either. It's just that when the others get mail and I don't, it hurts my feelings – and I feel like a little boy who has just dropped his lollipop in the mud! There's no reason to think up any more boloney to write. I devote most of my spare time to thinking of you and our love and future happiness. I love you.

November 1, 1943

Today marks the beginning of a new month of my sentence – or, what is more important, it completes an old month that is past and that brings our eventual reunion 30 days nearer. And that's the day for me!

I really shouldn't be writing to you again tonight as there was another mail delivery this evening, and as usual, I got left at the post. It's hard to stay sore about it, though, as I want so badly to believe it is the result of poor delivery. There is always the hope that you've been writing fast and furiously and that I'll get a dozen letters all at one time. Good old tomorrow! Without a belief in "mañana", we'd never get over the hump. I guess I sound pretty disgruntled about mail but it is pretty discouraging to have mail call after mail call pass you up and have to watch all the others walk off with their letters. It is pretty easy during the resulting period of depression to feel like there must be some concrete reason for it, even though you won't let yourself believe it when your mind is more normal. I might forgive you for finding diversions that I wouldn't approve and I could understand that your love for me could waver after our long separation – but I'd never forgive you if you didn't tell me about it and just let me go on pouring my heart out to you day after day.

I have realized that the reason I write you so often is that I lack the skill with words to express exactly how I feel and have to make up for my inability by just trying to impress you by the sheer volume of my "I love you's". The scrawniest cat, after looking upon the king, can only say "meow", and the grandeur he has seen has not increased his articulateness at all. So when I look upon our love, I can still only say "I love you" – but I can at least say it often and in a few different ways.

For God's sake, please write every now and then even if you just write and say you don't love me any more. This endless wait, wait, wait is the most nerve-wracking torture I have ever encountered in my life and I sometimes think I just can't stand it any more. And that's not a joke. I love you.

November 2, 1943

I only write this letter from the sheerest business necessity since I have sworn that I will not write any more letters to you except in answer to those I receive in the future, if any. Even to write a business letter to you has caused me to upset all my scruples, so I will ask you before you read further to cooperate with my stern desires and refuse to get any sort of pleasure from reading it. Of course, I'm joking. I guess if I found out you had absconded with Gayle and all my money to live with a draft dodger, I'd still have to write you almost every night. Your letters to me have been my greatest pleasure over here and I think my writing to you has been my next best.

I guess that's the reason it hurts me so badly for mail to come again tonight and me still not get any. Tommie Driggers got three V's, and he only corresponds with his wife. I realize you all are writing but I flat can't understand why my mail seems to be the only mail in the squadron that gets delayed. It's silly, I know, but I have been terribly upset the last few days because of it.

I am real proud of the nice, smooth envelopes I am using these days. They all stick together here, even before we get them, and we have to pry the flaps open with varying degrees of bad luck. I finally got smart and left all mine out one rainy night. The moisture softened the gum up, and I was able to open them fairly well then next morning. I stuck strips of oiled paper that cigaret cartons are wrapped in between the flap and the envelope and so have solved the problem. Of course, some dumb GI has probably been doing the same thing all the time but I'm still going to believe I was smart to think of it. Hell, I've got to keep my morale up somehow!

We had a little excitement the other day. Got in a new shipment of shirts and found a boxful that had built-in brassieres! Boy, was that something! The boys got a big laugh from it.

Please write as often as you can. It is real hell not to hear, and I'd give a hundred dollars for a V-mail right now! I love you so goddam much that I almost can't stand not hearing. Well, it'll all be over some day. I love you.

November 3, 1943

This will have to be another business letter as there was another mail delivery today and I still did not get any. I'll be damned if I am willing to write you any personal letters. After all, I have only had my pride and my mail over here – and, now that I only have my pride, I must cherish it lest I lose that too! Fortunately, it only took me a couple of hours to dig up an excuse for a "business" letter.

I am sending two packages. One contains my camera, which is coming a little "unstuck" from the moisture here. It will be very easily repaired and I want you to have it done as soon as you get the package because it is a very good camera. You can use it to take some more pictures of yourself and Gayle for me. Then I can take your picture and show it around and say, "Hey fellers! You remember that woman I used to sleep with at Fort Clark? I'm sure glad I never married her because she won't even write to me!"

I miss you so much, Virginia, and I love you both.

November 8, 1943 (noon)

There is a new rumor out – this one is to account for our shortage of mail – and it certainly illustrates the ability of troops to produce rumors to suit the needs of the day. It seems that certain h.a. (higher authority) has consistently refused to let the Navy send outgoing mail on Army planes, so the Navy has retaliated by refusing to bring in our mail on their boats, thereby reducing our mail to V's by air. This is an unusually good rumor, not because I believe it but because it at least fits the facts. We still haven't had any letter mail for a month and the Navy got 225 sacks yesterday.

We had another guy go nuts night before last. It was up in the second squad this time. The boy ran out of his tent hollering, "Bring 'em around again, Hooper!" and "Drill, you bastards," and "Stick 'em in the back, Wimberly," and a bunch of other cracks the soldiers have devised among themselves to express their opinions of certain people and their activities and characteristics. It took two hours to get him quiet and I heard they finally had to anesthetize him. I guess the boy just realized how little our dismounted drill and stove polishing were hurting the Japs.

Pardon me, but I just heard I have some mail! I love you.

November 9, 1943 V-mail

I was ashamed of myself after I got your letters last night but I must confess that I went to sleep happier than I have been in a long, long time.

There has been a time in our lives when I would have resented your proving yourself as being more magnanimous than

I am; I suppose because my old false pride would have resented it. I can only feel a sense of pride in you now, though, and a pleasant sense of security in knowing I have such a thoroughly generous and loyal lover. I don't begrudge you a penny that you need for any remotely reasonable pleasure, nor do I want you to account to me for everything you buy. To be frank, I would be bored if you filled your letters with, "I spent 69 cents on a fur-lined, overstuffed douche bag. I hated to do it, but my old one was just worn out."

This is the last sheet of paper I have so I'll make this short. I feel sure we will be home by summer and I promise that I'll do all I can to make up for the hardships and heartaches that our separation and my thoughtlessness has caused you. I love you.

November 15, 1943 (afternoon)
I do feel that I am the most fortunate man in the world to have a wife who suits me to such a high degree of perfection. I even enjoy fussing with you – and that's no faint praise! I think our greatest asset has been our ability to acquire enthusiasm to match each other's interests. Maybe I'll even learn to play bridge after I get home! (Please burn this letter!)

I really got a break this morning. We got a few PX supplies and "prorated" them among us as nearly as we could. I got a nice Ronson lighter with extra flints and fluid, a pocket comb, shaving mirror, 4 bars of milk chocolate, a flashlight, and a few small articles. And, miracle of miracles, I got a large bottle of shaving lotion – enough to last till I get my Christmas things!

I am probably as interested and almost as curious about your Christmas present. I selected three different gifts for you and gave them each a priority. If the first isn't available, then you get the second, etc. (No, you don't get all three!) And remember that if you think you can add $50 or $100 to your gift and get a gift of the same nature more suitable to you, don't hesitate to do so.

So, you can relax now. The whole thing is completely out of my hands, and I'll quit ranting so much about it. I have so little control over things from here and am so anxious for them to go just right that I've tried to take care of every contingency. Old maid, they call him! The frustrated perfectionist in person, I guess.

I just went to supper and got the surprise of my life. Six letters came in for me – and five were from you. It's incredible. I'm beginning to think you may love me after all. They were dated October 22, 23, 24, 25 and 27. (What were you doing October 26?) I never was so pleased in all my life to get so many consecutive letters. They're much more interesting that way although they are equally welcome no matter how or when I get them.

I will say that you took my cranky letters like a gentleman, and I appreciate it. I was wrong and my letters were way beyond the justification I had.

I have nothing fit to read and plan a quiet evening of drawing for a change. I've read every letter twice and I'm sure that if you could know what they mean to me, you'd not begrudge me a minute of them. They really help out, no fooling! I love you.

November 15, 1943

Col. Miller just called me in and told me that Rupert was gone (he's actually at the hospital awaiting evacuation), that it appeared he is leaving for good and I would remain in command of the squadron. At breakfast this morning Rupert told everyone how he got to be squadron CO at my expense. If I could give him credit for the subtlety, I would think he did it to irritate or embarrass me. He told it as a joke on Cunningham, and I guess that's the way he meant it.

I really think I got the best of the deal anyhow, as it has been pretty rough on him since he was in the position of having been thrust on Cunningham who has really never liked him. I am getting it back now and won't see Cunningham twice a month if that often. I have drawn more pay than he has for the entire period on account of my four years extra service. He's made the mistakes and gotten the blame and I've been able to look on in a more or less detached way and, I hope, profited by the things I've seen.

I know you will take good care of Gayle through the winter months. It scares me every time I think of her recent illness and really makes me want to be there to stand guard over her. That's a pretty silly reason for wanting to come home, as I know she gets every care possible. I guess we just tend to grasp at every reason over here to justify our constant desire to be with our wives and children.

Your letter a day idea is really wonderful. I have sense enough to know there will be days when you are completely lost for subject matter and other days when your burdens will not allow the time or strength. It is enough for me to know you are writing every day that you can.

I know how you hate to eat in the morning but I have learned that breakfast is the most important meal of the day. I never fail to eat something even though it may be pretty unattractive. The human body just wasn't made to run from 5:30 one night until noon the next day without any fuel. I'll make this deal: I'll get up and cook breakfast every morning if you'll get up and eat it with me. That'll be my concession to housekeeping and I think it is generous. (Of course, you know I'm kidding, as I really like to cook as you well know.)

I still feel my chances of being home by midsummer are very good. We are all waiting for the day they hit New Britain. It is obvious from the news commentators that that is our real objective and the day they start working on it will be the "beginning of the end" out here. New Britain is the last link in the chain of protection for Australia. If anyone over there has the idea that the Australians don't do their part of the fighting, and do it very well, they're badly informed. It's just too bad they had so many of their troops in North Africa when the Japs started this way.

I am sure all three of us agree that it is time for me to shut up and go to bed. Take care of yourself and my baby for me and keep up the good work on the letters. I love you.

November 21, 1943

I finished a letter up tonight that I started yesterday and mailed it to you. Will have to write another now, though, as I just hit the best jackpot on mail I have ever had because so many of the letters were from you. I got 11 letters.

Mrs Driggers wrote me a nice letter thanking me for the things I've done for Tommie. I am at a loss as to what it is I've done for him but appreciated the letter anyhow. As you know he has always been a considerable asset to me and certainly saved my hide on property when I had a troop, so anything I have been able to do for him has been little enough.

He just called me over to his tent for a big cup of cocoa. He's a better cook than Verner and would have been my mess sergeant instead of Murray except that I needed him worse as supply sergeant. Nothing is as good in big lots as when made in ordinary quantities, so he gets up and makes us coffee at 5:45 and I have a hot cup waiting when I get up at 6 every morning. And he makes cocoa every night at 9. Certainly helps to piece out the sorry rations we're getting these days, too.

I still think we'll have left by the time six or seven months have passed. I have gradually improved my "quarters" (sounds elegant, doesn't it?) to the point that I'd rather stay put than go anywhere except home. I don't think anyone could get acclimated here, but you can learn to endure, and I guess I have.

I am organizing a softball team out of my detachment plus the squadron medical detachment. They have about 15 men between the two groups and, with 10 men on a team, we can't pick just the "stars" – they all have to play. Of course, with 150 men, each troop can probably outplay us – but they can't have more fun! Kessler is a pretty good athlete and I think I have finally found something that will cheer him up a little. We have to go all the way to the strip to play but it is worth it.

Mama made a tactical mistake when she sent me the picture postcard of the Mineral Wells USO We just don't give a good goddamn about our poor, lonesome boys at home. Hell, don't they get steak and potatoes? From here that seems like all you could ask for. I wish they'd do a little more for my boys who deserve it instead of spending so much over there primarily to impress the parents. We don't even get good films.

It is 12 o'clock, my lantern has been lit for two hours, I am slowly going blind, I worked like hell today and see a repeat performance for tomorrow, so if you'll pardon me, I'll bid a quiet goodnight and go to bed.

I won't quit yet and leave this blank page when it is so easy to tell you I miss you every moment. Write as often as you can but don't overburden yourself. And never forget that I love you.

November 21, 1943 – V-mail

This is just a "pre-breakfast note" to tell you again that I love you. Makes it pretty conclusive, I think; you know how hard it is to love anybody before you've even had a cup of coffee! Actually, I didn't sleep very well last night and occupied my time with thoughts of you, Gayle and home in general, so you are in my thoughts this morning even more than usual.

I think from Thanksgiving until Christmas will be the hardest period so far in my separation from you. I sincerely believe that I'll be home for my next Thanksgiving. I couldn't stand a third one away from all of you. My motto is, "Home by July". That makes 24 months and I've put that as my quota. Don't know how MacArthur feels about it though. I love you.

November 24, 1943

I really got in on the mail again today with a postcard and four letters. That puts me to within three weeks of what gives at home and, as you know, that is pretty good.

I had Gary Cooper, Una Merkel and Phyllis Brooks for lunch today. They were over here doing some shows yesterday and today and wanted to get in a mess line and eat from mess kits, so we fixed them up. I don't know who picked on us to feed them – I didn't even get to go to the show.

We opened our officers' club today and had a reception for them. I got Cooper's autograph on a £1 note. That made it cost $3.23. I hope you'll think it was worth it! That was all the paper I had. Too bad I didn't take some of this Australian toilet paper that they issue us, as it is practically indestructible. Gayle may like it someday (the autograph, I mean; nobody could like the paper!)

I think of you both constantly and love you very much.

December 5, 1943

Confusion "rains" supreme – and me without a raincoat! We've been resolving chaos into order (and vice versa) for so long that no problem should stop us for long.

I believe another 90 days will complete MacArthur's primary objective and see a complete ring of protection around Australia. It seems a little tough to realize that, after two hard years, we have just managed to secure Australia, doesn't it? And really haven't touched the Japs seriously. It is too bad the people at home can't realize how things are and settle down to a long, hard effort.

Surprisingly enough, I have never slept better in my life than I do here. The nights are like late spring or early fall even to having dew on the ground every morning.

I can't overemphasize my happiness at the news of your newfound activity with the "service" girls. I think it will furnish that outside interest you have been needing so badly these past few months. I want you to feel free to outfit yourself adequately for the meetings, luncheons, parties (if any).

I hope you got the baby chair at Montgomery Ward's. It's hard to realize how scarce things are over there. I don't know why we can't understand it, though, as everything is certainly scarce enough here – and has been for 17 months. Of course, I mean things over and beyond the bare essentials necessary to live and to fight.

I'll be the first to agree that each of us is abnormal in one way or another and that we will grow more so as time passes, especially those who have some inherent weakness of mind or character. I read an article on the problems of soldiers returning to their families and will quote: "In addition to the strain of experiences he has been through, he has to face the psychological difficulties of returning to his family and home from which he may have been absent for three years. During these years of absence, he has had only the most limited contacts with his family. This situation tends to make his re-entry into family life a period of emotional and mental strain." I suppose it is a godsend that we can't look into the future too closely and see the heartbreaks that are ahead of us.

The ants are pretty bad here, worse than we had before, and I mildly suggested that Kessler get some insect powder and spread it around. When I came back from lunch, the inside of my tent looked like the inside of a freshly white-washed hen house – and I'm not exaggerating! I do have to admit though, that the ants are gone! I hate to have powder all over blankets, pillow, clothing, etc., but guess that is part of what I pay for getting this lovely chance to see the world. (Don't ask me to laugh, as I can't afford to risk having hysterics.)

Please believe that I want you to fix yourself up and enjoy the other service girls and their entertainments. We mustn't both be old and worn out when the war is over, you know, and I'll need your enthusiastic support to "recoup" as I'll be a little pooped out.

Sorry I couldn't answer all your letters before I tore them up. Don't think I missed anything vital as I reread them and noted the things I wanted to be sure to mention. I need to keep notes on what to write to you about. When I think of you, I only think of how much I ache for you and how much I love you.

December 12, 1943

I really feel as though I am finally cured from my drawn-out spell of defeatism and pessimism in general. The last five or six weeks have been the toughest I've ever seen on my frail spirits. I wasn't sure I was cured until the mail came tonight and I, as usual lately, did not get any. I said to hell with it, I've got two letters from you that I still can have the fun of answering. I really think I've got my second wind now and can tear off another few months of this monotony.

I don't know what really snapped me out of it. As you could tell from my letters (I hope), I was becoming a great deal more cheerful even before I got some mail the other day. That's one reason I feel like my cure is an artificial or temporary one induced by the stimulation of your two letters. The difference between being happy or depressed here is so minute that it isn't of much consequence. My real regret is that I wrote you a few unpleasant and depressing letters that I didn't mean and for which I have no material excuse. I know better than to say things that can't be retracted or that can be misinterpreted without my being there to correct them. It was pure damned carelessness and thoughtlessness on my part and I can't beg you enough to forget the whole thing.

I am scared to death that you may be disappointed and not get your Christmas present. I have heard that what I wanted you to have hasn't been in production since the war started. The manufacturer still advertises in a normal manner though, and I'm keeping my fingers crossed! Of course, the money won't rot if we have to keep it a while – but, hell, I send you money every month! Or, anyhow, the Finance Officer does. (You haven't started writing him instead of me, have you?) Have an alert on tonight. Better close. I love you,

December 17, 1943 – V-mail

I guess Christmas is over now (when you get this). We just had our fireworks a little early. Tommie and Kessler are with me and doing fine. Anything you've heard about Ed Wright being injured is not true – or certainly wasn't last night when I saw him. We have been very fortunate so far in our current endeavors. Would have liked it to be better, of course, but you can't bake a cake without breaking eggs. I sure hope you get this before Christmas as I want Gayle's first Christmas to be a happy one, and I'll be there to see that the rest of them will be! Don't worry about me. I am safe. I love you.

December 27, 1943 – V-mail

I'm ashamed of my failure to write when I know you are so worried about us but my "flu" turned out to be dengue fever and I am literally "sweating it out". I get up every morning with about 3° of fever and it gradually goes down until at night I don't have any. Next day it all starts over again. I can pick the damnedest times to get sick! Fortunately, we are momentarily caught up on our work and it hasn't hurt anything. The doctor says I'll be OK in a few days and there's not much to do for dengue over here except try to outlive it. Our boys continue to be fortunate and are getting on pretty well. We're just hoping the good luck holds out for them, as they're not in an enviable position. Write soon. I love you.

Dearest Virginia

Dearest Virginia:
I've been sitting here for an hour
and ... ted in a new detective
I have been able to think about ...
... you – so I might as well
... write you a letter and
... times, when I look ...
... end ...

1944

January 2, 1944

Well, another New Year has passed with me in the hospital, as usual. If I get stuck for a third Christmas and New Years overseas, my morale will sure be going to the dogs! I don't believe I can stand more than one more year of this or any more dengue fever. Actually, I'm counting strong on our getting to come home after New Britain is in the bag. I would give everything I own to arrive in the T&P station this afternoon to start a 30 day leave! It would be just too wonderful. But all that is idle fancy as we are going the other way as hard as we can and home never seemed further away. It is pleasant to sit here in the jungle heat and think of ice cream and cold Coca-Cola and real, honest-to-god steak and potatoes – lettuce, tomatoes and mayonnaise! Or even a hotdog or hamburger with Fritos (this corned beef is killing me!).

No, this dengue fever hasn't got me nuts, at least no nuttier than usual. In fact, except for being a little weak, I feel unusually good.

I wrote the foregoing this afternoon and it is now 9:30 p.m. We are showing a picture for our detachment tonight but I chose to stay home and rest a little due to my recent fever. Boy, did I have an experience! I was laying on my bunk with my hands at my side and was about half asleep when I felt something touch my hand. Sort of felt like a dog's cold nose. I instinctively brushed it aside and heard a "plop" on the floor like someone had dropped a short length of rope. I threw my flashlight down there and there was a nice 3½ to 4 foot brown jungle snake with the perfect triangular head of a poisonous snake! It was apparently coming up the side of the bed and was insecure when its head touched my hand, hence it falling so easily when I brushed it away. My pistol was in my footlocker of all places and I couldn't find a stick before it had gotten away, so I guess it is still around. Will I have fun sleeping now!

Of course, such a thing wouldn't happen over once in a lifetime. In fact, that is the first snake I have ever seen in New Guinea on either trip so there's no use in your starting to worry about snakes as well as everything else. I'll just be careful to tuck my mosquito bar in from now on when I lie down and that will settle that. I told you about it because it was something different and also because it would pass the censor. Most of the things I get into these days wouldn't, you know, and that makes writing a little hard for me.

It's late, so will close for now. I would give anything to be home. I love you.

January 5, 1944 – V-mail

I sure seem to be hoodooed on your mail – don't know why it takes so long to hear from you, except that my impatience makes it seem longer. There really is little excuse for writing a letter tonight except the usual that I am lonely and heartsick for you and just can't seem to go to sleep without writing. I don't think I remembered to tell you all about our earthquake the other day. It occurred while I was in the hospital and I guess I overlooked it.

Beside, the earthquake isn't particularly big stuff with us these days. Anyhow, it lasted for a period of over a minute, shook the trees badly and made water in the ruts and foxholes slosh a bit. I guess we might as well get used to them as I understand they are more and more prevalent as you move on up from island to island. I slept all afternoon and really feel fine. I love you.

January 9, 1944 – V-mail

Well, "another day, another dollar" as we used to say. The general has made the statement that he was going to try to get us home after this mess is over. We hope he'll stick to it. Of course, most of us are original, charter members of the Skeptics Society. Nevertheless, we cling to such little hopes like drowning men clutching at match sticks. I guess our greatest hope is in Russia pushing on to Germany so our troops in Europe can pull a quick victory march through Berlin and then come out here to fight. I love you.

January 11, 1944 – V-mail

I am sorry to have had to miss writing yesterday but I was suddenly notified in the morning to pack up and move back here as Task Force S-4 which, as you know, is a supply job. I was a little disappointed although my best judgment tells me that it is much safer back here. That doesn't make you like leaving the guys you have been soldiering with for several years just when the water starts getting hot. Anyhow, here I am on a completely strange job. I think I can handle the job OK but it is somewhat of a responsibility as I have to send them everything they get and some of the items are on the critical list, as you can imagine. We have regular bombing raids around here but none seem to come near our headquarters, and it seems about as safe as we were last summer, even though we are a good deal nearer our little yellow friends.

I didn't relish another barge trip across waters of such questionable control but my luck has remained unshaken (knock, knock). It seems like I've been sort of a guinea pig for the past eight or nine months in that every time they start to get control of a new gulf or sea, they send me across it once or twice just to make sure.

The Russian news is wonderful, and we are delighted that somebody is doing something substantial to Germany besides bombing them from the air. It looks like the beginning of the end, although the Germans may be able to delay them long enough to set up a strong line to take cover behind when they get back to their own borders. I don't really think they'll have a lot of luck at that sort of thing.

We've been hearing about Congress passing a law giving us furloughs after so many months in the malarial zone but we don't want any furloughs. We just want to serve whatever length of time we have to serve away from home and come home for good. I can't understand why they don't get busy and start sending a few troops over here and replace us rather than messing with some sort of furlough business. It would at least serve to keep the various units intact. And, of course, we believe that any man that has put in two years out here has done his share – at least as long as there are five to seven million USC Commandos still at home who haven't done anything. It isn't hard to understand why they are reluctant to let soldiers vote!

Write soon and remember *all the time* that I love you.

January 12, 1944 – V-mail

Am having a good time getting into my new work, largely because I am so glad to have a job to do where I don't feel comparatively useless. We have occasional night bombings none of which have been in the immediate area, and I feel pretty secure. There were a couple too close for comfort when I was in the hospital but that is some distance away from where I am now. Am camped on a beach under some lovely trees and the tent stays in the shade all the time. Had time for an hour's nap today after lunch that helped regain some of the sleep I lost while I was with the rest of the boys en route there and back. That en route part is what made me nervous, incidentally, as I don't even have a life preserver. I think this job will become simpler and simpler as time goes on although something new seems to pop up every day. I really like it though. I love you.

January 19, 1944 – V-mail

I got moved up to the new headquarters today. I really like the new set up and have an office – well, that's what you call it when you can't do better – and a clerk, with Kessler as major domo, whatever that is. A hell of a nice bunch of guys here and I really am enjoying the new contacts as I meet people from all over the country.

We had fresh meat the other day for the first time since November. Of course, you always get fresh meat when you travel with the Navy as they seem to have an endless supply. Their edge on us is that they have refrigeration and can take care of it whereas we have to dribble it out as best we can and we can only get a day's supply delivered to us at a time because if we held it over without refrigeration it would spoil.

You can probably tell that I am just stalling to think of something to write about. I guess I am just tired from moving as that is always a task when you don't have enough men handy.

I think I am getting to the point where words are inadequate. I want to come home! Need I say more? I love you.

January 23, 1944 – V-mail

Our G-3 at this headquarters is Col. Archie Roosevelt, Teddie's youngest son and brother to Kermit. My work requires that I spend some of the time with him on occasions and he is really a right guy. Mildest man you ever saw but appearances are completely deceiving as he holds the Croix de Guerre. He was written up in Nov. 27th copy of *Time* magazine for his courage.

It is actually the 24th, as I started this last night but was interrupted by our little yellow friends in big airplanes. Can't give you the details as yet but will send them as soon as they are announced in the papers. Not much damage was done and all the injuries were just scratches received by guys diving for foxholes. I am unscathed purely because I had no hole to dive at. I'm correcting that though!! I got a ditch digging machine from an engineer friend of mine and we are completely surrounding our area with 5 ft. deep ditches. The machine is the type ordinarily used to lay pipe lines so you can imagine how effective it is.

I still enjoy my work here. Everyone is pleasant and reasonable in every respect and it is certainly a happy change. (These damn V-mails are too short for me.) I love you.

January 24, 1944 – V-mail

This is another of those delayed jobs as it is now the morning of the 25th. We have had so many alerts lately (most of them false) that I just can't get much done at night. We've had a few bombs fall lately out of a clear sky and without any forewarning at all. Some of the "green" troops camped about us give the signal for an alert every time they hear an outboard motor. Most of us are calloused to danger by now and disregard indications until we get the official warning – except, of course, when the bombs fall before the warning is sounded. Personnel is always a secondary target as the Japs much prefer to bomb ships, docks and air strips, so we really are not in a great deal of danger. Hope to stay here for a while.

I saw Ed the other day. He was evacuated to the hospital here and from here back to Australia. He just hadn't recovered from the nervous trouble he had on Woodlark and the "rubber boat" episode was too much for him. He is perfectly normal in every way and there is nothing wrong with his mind at all. He has simply had a nervous breakdown. (I am being specific because I am sure some long-tongued Dallas sister will start a rumor that he had lost his mind or something.)

You complain of no sunshine and I regret that I can't divvy up with you as I have enough for both of us and a little to spare. It is really hot up here and is due to get hotter before the wind changes, and then it gets rainy again. Actually, we have two kinds of weather here – hot or hot and wet. You can't imagine how I'd enjoy a real good shiver! It would probably give me pneumonia, though. I love you.

January 30, 1944 – V-mail

I have received several letters and eight boxes from all of you in the last two days – model stuff, food (such as olives, etc.), and from Gayle, my most precious gift – shaving lotion (precious because it was from Gayle and because it was the thing I wanted more than anything else I got).

Incidentally, Col. Roosevelt said to thank you for that caviar. I don't eat it, but he's quite an epicure and got a great kick out of sitting in a native shed on the beach under coconut trees eating Russian caviar! I'm really glad you sent it as I laughed at him for 30 minutes. I couldn't have had nearly so much fun if I had eaten it myself. Well, these are still too short, aren't they? Write often. I love you.

February 5, 1944

Kessler got a nice package from a girl this morning and we all crowded around and made so much of it that the poor kid nearly cried. He certainly gets as little from home as anyone and he is so proud that it hurts him to be left behind in the package sweepstakes. He got a swell identification bracelet and a number of toilet articles. Really cheered the kid up especially since all of us made such a to-do about it. He's a good boy but sure gets despondent at times. Not a great deal I can do about it although he gets a big kick out of me bringing the big shots over to his tent for cocoa every night.

We really had a funny thing happen yesterday. I was driving along a road parallel to an air strip yesterday and the major riding with me said, "Look at those damn fools making practice runs at their foxholes." Just as I looked around to see the "practice run", a nice, big, fat bomb landed just close enough to scare the hell out of us and not close enough to hurt anything but our feelings. (PS We decided the guys were not practising.)

I don't want you to worry, though. I firmly believe that nothing will stop me getting home to you and Gayle. I love you.

February 7, 1944

After writing the V-mails to you last night, I put on my new pajamas and stretched out to read a bit. The pajamas are swell if for no other reason than because I am more or less restricted to the bunkhouse after I put them on and can't get up and fidget around all evening. They are also cool and comfortable and, best of all, I can hop up and hightail it to a slit trench without stopping to dress – just slip on my shoes now and tear out. Quite an improvement and also a sort of insurance as we by no means get warned before the Japs come in, and even when we do get a warning, it is usually pretty damned short.

Willie Phillips was running along beside a tank during an attack and it knocked two trees down on him. He was in the hospital here a few days. Was pretty badly beaten up, but I think he will come out OK.

Speaking of bombing, I saw a really beautiful sight recently. I had been in bed reading and went outside to wash my hands. Just as I went out the door, I looked up and saw two planes coming in by the moonlight. They were really pretty with the moonlight reflected. I almost forgot to holler "lights out" and just called everyone outside to look. About that time, our searchlights picked them up and we ran for our trench. The lights kept them in sight for the entire period they were over us and the tremendous AA fire really made a 4th of July show. We kept gaping even while the flak was dropping all around us. It was the best show I've seen since I've been overseas. We are sure they were hit as we could see the tracers and shell bursts all around them. However, neither of them fell while they were in sight and both completed their bombing runs.

It appears I am to be "requisitioned" by this outfit to join their staff as an Asst. G-4. I didn't ask for the job at all and am pleased that they like my work well enough to want me. I've always said that an officer who could even get by in a cavalry regiment satisfactorily would find anything else to be easy, and I am finding that I was right. The CO of this outfit is an ex-governor of South Dakota. He is only subordinate to General MacArthur and is as good a soldier as we used to think he was at Fort Clark when he was making inspection trips down there.

Tell the folks about the "air show". I love you.

February 24, 1944 – V-mail

Our situation around here has improved to an almost incredible degree of late, and we hardly know what an air alert sounds like. I don't think it is just a temporary thing, either, although it is still perfectly possible for the Japs to whip over any time they like. It just seems that since the attack on Truk, they are busy elsewhere. I'm sure they haven't forgotten us entirely but it is a relief not to have to get up two or three times every night and run to a slit trench.

I am glad Hare's wife is taking his death so bravely. He is the only officer loss we have had whose family was known to me. As one Dallas officer put it (pretty callously, I thought), his family will live better off a pension than from any income he was apt to make for them. I can't imagine that is any particular consolation to them, however. And it certainly doesn't help Hare any!

I have a piece of Japanese money – a bill – and will send it to you via Dad as I think he might enjoy showing it around at work. Galloupe took it off one of them and thought you might like it. Don't know whether you remember him or not but he was the big, ugly horseshoer that we called Arkansas.

As you know by now, I got over the dengue fever alright. Of course, after you've had all the things we've had out here, I don't suppose you really completely recover and I am still 15 or 20 pounds lighter than I was when we left Clark. I hope to regain it on the way home and think a little time in a cool climate will make me as good as new. Right now I feel pretty much secondhand, though.

Hope I get home during a warm time of year because I honestly don't believe that I could stand winter without a chance to gradually become accustomed to it. I certainly wouldn't have a stitch of clothing fit to wear in the USA. All the cottons I have are threadbare and whitened from so much hand laundering with GI soap. Guess I could pick up a suntan shirt or two and a pair of slacks in SF for about $30. Would have to have new ones anyhow as I only have the one shirt and two pairs of slacks now that my present clothing is worn out. If I don't get home until winter, then that situation is automatically OK as I sure have plenty of wool stuff. I would have to get back into a horse outfit to keep from wasting the fancy breeches. That would mean a choice between Gen. Johnson and the 124th. I say to hell with the breeches! I love you.

Letters from the end of February to the beginning of May 1944 are missing from my mother's carefully preserved archive.

May 17, 1944

Things have taken a sudden turn for the better and this will be the last note from me for a couple or three days. I'm sure you will be as glad as I am that I have to write it in haste.

You don't know how thoroughly happy I am to know that I am actually starting the long trip back to you. And how glad, too, that I can come to you just as I left and without an apology for any thought or deed of mine since I saw you last.

My thoughts today are centered upon my love for you, my pride in our happy marriage and in our daughter. I don't feel like being over-elaborate. I think you know what I mean without my going further. Until I can write again (you may not get them when I do write as they may come on the same ship), remember I love you.

June 2, 1944

I still have had no mail and really can't expect any yet. I go to the post office and ask every day just the same. I am sure the 112th is forwarding my mail here by now, and I should hear directly from you within the next week or so.

Our little flurry of excitement has died down, as might have been expected. Only the quota from the combat units is here now, and we have finally found out that we can't begin to leave until the other forces (supply and Air Force ground units) decide to send their quotas. Of course, it is hard to reconcile the delay.

We have so many things to reconcile, however, that I guess it would eventually run us nuts if we kept on trying to rationalize our situation. New officers arriving here, many of whom have already had foreign service, claim they were rushed over so fast that they couldn't tell their families goodbye. And here they are, sitting and waiting to be moved on north just as we are waiting to come on home. Since there is no lack of transportation, it is hard to justify their wait here with the rush to get them over.

We were first told that we had no immediate hope of rotation since we were needed so badly. Then they told us we were still too short on troops to spare more than a "token" number. Our delay here has already been six weeks long and appears that it will be at least that much longer.

Of course, it would be a simpler problem for us if we were still with our units and doing something even remotely connected with winning the war. Here, as I have told you, we are not even in daily contact with the war news much less near any but the most nominal military activities. And we have no part in those. I would estimate the nearest Japs to be more than 1000 miles from here – and that is conservative.

There is an easy explanation of the whole thing, of course, but I am hesitant to accept it even though it comes most nearly to covering the situation. I don't want to accept it primarily because I prefer to last out the rest of the war without becoming bitter.

This theory – and it is believed by many – is that they have never really intended to have an effective rotation policy in this theater in the first place. But so far I am rejecting this theory because it would obviously lower my respect for the service and destroy my morale. I think I have managed to stay as happy and cheerful and willing as most. And I am ready now to do anything here, however menial, if it will help to accomplish what I came into the service to do – namely, to win the war.

I suppose I would take a different attitude entirely if I were a member of the Regular Army and had the assurance of a lifetime income, adequate for a better than average standard of living. Unfortunately, I have to come back some day and start to work in competition with younger men who will have good health and the enthusiasm of beginners. I knew this when I came into the Army but could not conscientiously let any such consideration keep me from doing what I considered my duty. Now that I find they can carry on the war to their satisfaction and leave so many of us in idleness over here, it is only natural that I feel they could very well discharge me and get me back to a gainful occupation where I can be doing something for myself, if not for my country. As it is, I am doing nothing for either.

I think we were happier at first when we thought the delay was caused by indifference or inefficiency on the part of a few subordinates somewhere. Now that we feel it is a result of rules laid down by the War Department, it is far harder to understand. What conceivable good can we be doing as we just sit and wait for specially earmarked replacements since we are not with our units and are completely out of the scheme of the war?

I came into the Army when I was told to and took no advantage of the loopholes as many did. I came overseas when I was ordered to without protest even though you were in ill health and pregnant. I have done what I was told to do when I was told to do it. I certainly can lay no claim to being a hero. On the other hand, I am equally sure that I have never shirked a duty, however tiresome or hazardous. I have stayed as healthy and as happy as it has been possible to stay under the circumstances; certainly, I have stood up as well as those about me.

I hope that I can continue this way. In fact, I feel sure that I can. It is necessary that I do if I am to come out of the service with my self respect intact and with my belief that it has all been worth while. As I see it, we will have as great a task after the war as we have now in fighting it. And if we are to protest our interests in either peace or war, it is necessary that we maintain at least an illusion that we are of some value to ourselves and our country. We can no more do this as cynics than it has been done by theorists during the past ten years or so.

Write to me soon, and remember that I love you and am longing for the day when I can be back home with you.

July 3, 1944

Today a year ago, I was within a mile of where I am right now loading the regiment out for our first amphibious landing. The intervening time has been, for the most part, the dullest stretch of my entire life. All of it has either been too dull or too exciting to be enjoyable. I think I preferred the exciting although there were plenty of times when I'd have given a lot to get one complete night's sleep without an air raid.

As I look back at the long and heartbreaking wait that I have been through since I last saw you, it seems sort of silly to be so anxious now. At worst, I have only a few more weeks to go – and I am sure of seeing you now. There have been times during the last two years when I wouldn't have bet a plugged nickel that I would ever see you again. It is hard to believe now when we are so utterly safe that I could have been so damned scared. Fortunately, we were too busy to worry a great deal at the time.

I have just come from the post office where, as usual, I didn't have any mail. I did have a letter from the Base Censor. Thought sure I was going to get to go up and defend some of my opinions, but it turned out that I had very carefully addressed a V-mail and mailed it – without writing any letter on it!!

I don't know whether that strikes you as funny or not, but we thought it was hilarious. I know people who have gotten in trouble for making milder statements than I have made to you – and then I get a letter returned because I had not written anything at all. Is that not funny – or has all this rain warped my sense of humor?

No matter how much I write I still can't express to you, even remotely, how much I love you nor how anxious I am to be with you. You will just have to deduce it from the fact that I spend at least two hours a day writing. Quantity is not as good as quality – but I hope it is worth a little bit. If the length of my letters does as much as hint to you the love and desire that prompts it, then they have been well worth the effort. I love you.

July 5, 1944

We got over the "Big 4th" with no apparent damage to us from over-celebration. As a matter of fact, it was amazing that we were so self-restrained! We did play a couple of hours of volleyball with the inevitable result of sore backs and legs today. But we can't lay that onto our exuberant patriotism as we did the same thing the day before.

I am still optimistic that we'll get out by the 15th. I have little reason to feel that way, but you have to have confidence in something.

The delay is still due to the failure of the Service of Supply to send their quota down. All the other barriers have been surmounted. Except, of course, that a vessel cannot be set aside to haul us home until they finally come out. Some fun!

We gripe so much that the games we play are doubly valuable. Not only do they keep our mind off this needless waste of trained manpower through delay, but also entertain us quite a bit. I don't know that we will get to play volleyball today as it is raining in a really comprehensive sense of the word. This is undoubtedly one of the wettest spots on earth – certainly at this time of year anyhow.

Even if we get out by the 15th – and we certainly are not sure of that – we can't get home in less than five or six weeks. Six weeks would put me in Fort Worth about September 1st. Another month for leave and reassignment makes it October 1st. Then if I only got to stay in the US for three months and another month travel back overseas, it would be December 1st before I could arrive in another theatre and several more months before I could see any real activity – say late next Spring. Hell, the war could easily be over by then.

It's time to go to the post office so I'll close and get this off. I still miss you as badly as ever – and sometimes worse! But there's no use repeating the same thing over and over again. I love you.

July 7, 1943

This game playing is really good for me, I think. When I was a kid, I was always delivering papers, magazines, milking a cow or something when the other kids played games in the afternoons. As a result, I never was too good at them and spent most of my spare time, eventually, in reading. No one really likes to do anything with a group that they don't do as well as the average – or better. Hence, I just kidded myself into believing that I just didn't care for people or games.

I know that I have always had an inferiority complex because I couldn't learn to compete with other kids years ago. The real excuse may be that I was inept but since I play them as well as others now, I think it was because I didn't have the time and chance to learn them like the others did. Kids have to learn by doing things. I play now by figuring the games out in my mind tactically – and kids' minds are too immature for that.

Of course, I know that I learned a few things that the other kids didn't, but not a great deal that anyone could not learn within a year after they went to work later on. The main thing I learned was to be independent financially (or to want to be) and that really just served to supplement the false security I built up to defend my inferiority complex.

I think that an error of many parents who are ambitious for their children is in trying to make their children into what they themselves would have liked to have been. Or to make them into something that they particularly admire. My ambition for Gayle is that she shall grow up to have an intelligent but uncomplicated mind in a healthy body because I'd rather she were happy than be a ballet dancer or a concert pianist. And I want her to learn to compete gracefully in youth. It is a little late to learn once you are grown. Well, I guess I'll stop my pseudo-psychology. Remember I love you.

July 10, 1944

We went up to the PX last night and I bought these tablets just for spite. I don't figure I'll write enough now to make any difference but I've been asking for airmail stationery for 60 days and been refused only to find last night that they kept it hidden and only sold it to the home guard. That sort of stuff sure burns me up, and the greatest satisfaction I've had overseas was the 5½ months I had at a supply base with enough prestige to make them give us the stuff that they'd always saved for their own use.

We are afraid to send any more laundry out now for fear we'll lose it. I have two of my four shirts in mine and would rather bring them home dirty than lose them. As a result, I am buying two cotton shirts although I hate to do it. But we can't wash stuff on the boat since we have only salt water in the tub and soap gums up in it and just won't lather. I tried to wash my hair one time and had to rinse it out under an ice water drinking tap. Some fun!

I am really thrilled at the idea that I will soon be on my way. It is almost inconceivable that anything can mess us up now. Of course, if we have to come in "shifts" as the April group did, I'll almost surely miss the first one. But it will only be a few days until we do get out after they leave. It won't be long. I love you.

July 11, 1944

This will be a little short as it will soon be time for the morning mail to get out and I wanted to get a letter off for sure.

We are losing one of our game group tonight as the AA Lt. Col. who has been playing with us is leaving. We hate to see him go but realize that his leaving is the best possible news for the rest of us.

I have spent the morning moving from my footlocker into a barracks bag and will be inconvenienced as hell for a day or so until our turn comes too, as we turn in our luggage (footlockers and bedrolls) this afternoon and don't get them back until we get to San Francisco.

I'll close and get this out. Hope I receive a letter from you today. That is all it would take to make this my Red Letter Day. I love you.

July 12, 1944

Well, I'm down to a point where there isn't a great deal to say. I have spent the day trying to learn to live out of a bag. I have packed the damned thing three times – and still find something on top that ought to be on the bottom – my field jacket and GI shoes, for instance. But this is no time to complain.

I got four cartons of cigarets today, my allowance for the next three weeks, more or less. I already had three cartons, so I am pretty well set for the trip. That should get me all the way to Fort Worth, and will, too, if I don't run into another stupid delay in San Francisco or somewhere.

I don't know how to arrange to meet you in El Paso. I feel sure we can get a room at the Hilton or the Paso del Norte. Unless we change our plans by phone from San Francisco, I'll call both hotels looking for you and leave a number where you can call me – or, better yet, why don't you wire for a reservation when you know what time you'll arrive, and I will not take a room at all? I'll just stay at the post until you get there. You can also wire me a "will call" message at Western Union (the Western

Union people in Fort Worth know what a 'will call' message is –
I suppose it is obvious). You can put in the time of your arrival
and I will meet your train if I get there first. If I don't meet it, then
you'll know I haven't arrived yet and can just go on to the hotel
and take up your reservation until I call.

There is no reason to expect us to have any rail delay after
I finally let you know when I leave San Francisco. We could be
delayed 24 or 36 hours en route, of course, but that is
improbable. And there isn't enough chance of it to think about it.
I just mention it so you won't be worried in case I'm a little later
than I figured.

I should be able to gauge the thing pretty closely by that
time, but you never can tell what the hell sort of screw ups the
Army can get into. And I guess the railroads are pretty well tied
up these days, too.

It is wonderful to think of our getting to meet on "neutral"
ground where we will know no one at all and can do as we
please. I'll be having a hard time keeping my hands off you the
first week or so. And I certainly don't want to be inhibited for the
first few days together. I'd rather we'd meet in an impersonal
hotel room than in some familiar place. After all, we'll be making
memories, not rehashing old ones. And we will make some
gorgeous ones, too.

I could go on for hours like this but would only be repeating
myself for the hundredth time. It is a little hard to write this last
letter, anyhow. Sort of like we felt on that last telephone call
before I went overseas.

I am keyed up and know I'll sleep but little tonight –
especially since I have my bedroll sealed and can't sleep on it.
Just have a bare cot and a couple of blankets – but I'd gladly sit
up all night, everything considered. I don't even care if my last
breakfast here is dehydrated eggs! (That's a real compliment to
you, believe it or not.)

The line represents a pause during which a detail came in and carried off our checkable baggage. I was glad to see mine go because it is a real milestone in my slow and torturous road home.

Several of the other fellows hang out here in our tent in their spare time so it is now pretty late and I need to get the light out so the others can sleep. I guess it's a good thing that something limits the length of my letters, else they'd run on and on like the proverbial (or is it poetical?) brook.

Well, it is now the morning of the 13th and I have to get this finished whether I like it or not – or else not mail it.

The beginning of the end is here and all our unhappiness will soon seem insignificant in the happiness of our reunion. I love you so very much that I can hardly contain myself. I love you.

(Don't forget the letters to San Francisco!!)

July 13, 1944 – V-mail

This is the supplement to my last letter. I haven't had breakfast yet but was a bit restless last night and got up about an hour too early. Guess that was because my bedroll and rubber mattress were gone. I don't mind, though, as I should be very comfortable before I go to bed tonight.

It will be about 2½ to 3½ weeks before you hear from me again, probably 21 days. I can't be any more exact than that. Wish I could. You can get yourself pretty well ready from what you already know – and the rest will just have to create a little suspense in your life. Personally, I expect to go completely nuts the last 24 hours before I land.

With all the time I have had to prepare myself, I just can't believe it is true that I'll soon be with you again. It is just too good to be true. Until you hear from me again, remember that I love you.

Lloyd.

Epilogue

My father wrote this poem towards the end of his time in New Guinea. It was inspired by a poem published in *Tall Talk from Texas* by Boyce House, one of his favourite books.

Somewhere on a South Sea island,
where the sun is like a curse,
And each day long is followed by
another, slightly worse.
Where the coral dust blows thicker
than the shifting desert sand
And a white man thinks and dreams
of a finer, cooler land.

Somewhere in the South Pacific,
where a woman is never seen,
Where the sky is never cloudy
where the grass is never green,
Where the birds always chatter, and
the rats crawl and squeak,
Where there isn't any whiskey,
and the beer is mighty weak.

Somewhere below the equator,
where the nights are made for love,
Where the moon is like a searchlight
and the Southern Cross above,
Sparkling stars are bright and many
in the warm, tropical night,
It's a shameless waste of beauty,
since there's not a girl in sight.

Somewhere in the South Pacific,
where the mail is always late,
Where Xmas cards in April
are considered up to date,
Where we always have a pay roll
but never have a cent,
We don't even miss the money, cause
we'd never get it spent.

Somewhere in the South Sea islands,
where the swirling frigates cry,
And the lumbering deep sea turtles
come up on the bank to die,
Oh, take me back to Texas,
the place I love so well,
for this God-forsaken island is a
Substitute for Hell.